HIGH-YIELD ROUTINES
for GRADES K–8

Ann McCoy
University of Central Missouri, Warrensburg, MO

Joann Barnett
Missouri State University and Ozarks Technical Community College, Springfield, MO

Emily Combs
Clinton Middle School, Clinton, MO

NATIONAL COUNCIL OF
TEACHERS OF MATHEMATICS

Library of Congress Cataloging-in-Publication Data

McCoy, Ann C., 1961-
  High yield routines / by Ann McCoy, University of Central Missouri, Warrensburg,
Missouri, Joann Barnett, Missouri State University, Springfield, Missouri, Emily Combs,
Clinton Middle School, Clinton, Missouri.
      pages cm
  ISBN 978-0-87353-719-3
  1. Mathematics--Study and teaching (Elementary) 2. Cognitive learning. I. Barnett,
Joann. II. Combs, Emily. III. Title.
  QA135.5.M45456 2013
  372.7--dc23
                              2013003553

The National Council of Teachers of Mathematics is the public voice of mathematics
education, supporting teachers to ensure equitable mathematics learning of the highest
quality for all students through vision, leadership, professional development, and research.

Printed in the United States of America

Contents

Introduction

1st grade   Claire, a first grader, enters her classroom and hangs her backpack in her assigned cubby. After placing her take-home folder on her desk, she moves to the front of the classroom. There she chooses a magnet in the shape of a banana and places it under the Brought Lunch heading to indicate she would not be eating school lunch since she brought a lunch from home.

3rd grade   Third graders Laurel and Cody are each working on a story about a favorite memory. When they hear their teacher say, "One, two," they stop working, look at her, and reply, "Eyes on you." She tells the class to move to their conferencing areas, so Laurel and Cody move to the couch—their assigned area for the week. After the conferencing time ends, Cody collects papers from the class.

7th grade   As seventh grader Andre enters the classroom, he picks up his math journal. The question of the day is posted on the board, and Andre begins composing a response to the question. After a few minutes, the teacher signals the students to put their journals away. Andre passes his journal to the right. When the pile of journals reaches the end of the row, the student sitting at the end places the pile back in the class tub.

Our classrooms are full of routines. Our students quickly learn the procedure for taking attendance and lunch count, the procedure for assigning classroom jobs, the procedure for lining up, and the procedure for collecting and distributing papers. The creation and implementation of routines brings a sense of predictability and comfort to our classrooms. Routines help with organization and classroom management, and they help make transitions smooth. Although we often think of routines as being used for organization, routines can also be used to enhance instruction.

Many textbooks make suggestions and give directions for a variety of mathematical routines. These mathematical routines are structured activities that, when used consistently, can help students gain proficiency with a range of concepts and practices. Some of these routines are well known and commonly implemented. One example is Calendar Time, a familiar and often-implemented routine described in textbooks as well as supplementary resources. Calendar Time allows students to learn about the months of the year, days of the week, and school-day activities through using the calendar (Shumway 2011). Teachers may also design questions, based on the calendar, that allow students to practice grade-specific skills. Whereas teachers use Calendar Time often, they use other routines less frequently, and as a result, many opportunities to enhance our students' understanding of and proficiency with mathematics are lost.

Consistent use of routines can yield many benefits for students. Such routines offer access to the big ideas of mathematics and allow deep understanding of concepts. In fact, routines can be designed to focus on the desired mathematical content. Mathematical routines also give students opportunities to develop expertise with the eight mathematical practices described in the Common Core State Standards for Mathematics (National Governors Association Center for Best Practices [NGA Center] and Council of Chief State School Officers [CCSSO] 2010; see fig. I.1 and the appendix). The mathematical practices are based on the National Council of Teachers of Mathematics (NCTM; 2000) Process Standards of Problem Solving, Reasoning and Proof, Communication, Representation, and Connections as well as the strands of mathematical proficiency described in the National Research Council's book *Adding It Up* (Kilpatrick, Swafford, and Findell 2001). Mathematical routines offer opportunities for students to demonstrate their thinking and for teachers to gain insight into the thinking of their students.

Standards for Mathematical Practice

1. Make sense of problems and persevere in solving them.
2. Reason abstractly and quantitatively.
3. Construct viable arguments and critique the reasoning of others.
4. Model with mathematics.
5. Use appropriate tools strategically.
6. Attend to precision.
7. Look for and make use of structure.
8. Look for and express regularity in repeated reasoning.

Fig. I.1.

The Standards for Mathematical Practice described in the Common Core State Standards for Mathematics (NGA Center and CCSSO 2010, p. 6)

turn and talk

Implementing mathematical routines can prove beneficial to students across all grade levels. In *Principles and Standards for School Mathematics*, NCTM (2000) calls for curriculum that is coherent and well articulated. A coherent curriculum is organized around important mathematical ideas so that students can see how the ideas build on and connect with other ideas. A well-articulated curriculum provides guidance regarding the important mathematical ideas that should be emphasized and the depth of study appropriate for each grade level As teachers from multiple grade levels plan and consistently implement common routines, students will experience a more coherent and better-articulated mathematical experience. In addition, the use of common models such as number lines and Venn diagrams within the routines will improve students' ability to accurately and strategically use these models.

Mathematical routines are easily and quickly implemented. Once developed, most routines will take five to ten minutes per day. The routines are commonly used at the beginning of a lesson, but they could also be implemented at the end of the lesson or even within a lesson. Choosing a few routines to implement and implementing them consistently and often will yield the greatest benefits for students.

In this book, we present seven easily implemented mathematical routines that may be used effectively at a variety of grade levels and with a variety of mathematical content. We also provide some ideas for infusing mathematics into the nonmathematical routines that take time away from instruction. Here are the titles of the remaining chapters:

Chapter 1: Today's Number

Chapter 2: Mystery Number

Chapter 3: Alike and Different

Chapter 4: Number Lines

Chapter 5: Quick Images

Chapter 6: Guess My Rule

Chapter 7: How Do You Know?

Chapter 8: Infusing Mathematics into Nonmathematical Routines

Chapter 9: High Yield from Routines

Each chapter begins with classroom vignettes that provide a glimpse of how the routine might look as it is implemented in a variety of grade levels. A description of the routine and implementation strategies follow. We give examples of student work from various grade levels for each of the routines, examples of ways to assess student thinking by using the routines, and suggestions for adapting the routines.

We hope the routines we describe and the student work we share will encourage you to try the routines with your own students and to think of creative ways to implement these and other mathematical routines.

References

Kilpatrick, Jeremy, Jane Swafford, and Bradford Findell, eds. *Adding It Up: Helping Children Learn Mathematics*. Washington, D.C.: National Academies Press, 2001.

National Council of Teachers of Mathematics (NCTM). *Principles and Standards for School Mathematics*. Reston, Va.: NCTM, 2000.

National Governors Association Center for Best Practices (NGA Center) and Council of Chief State School Officers (CCSSO). *Common Core State Standards for Mathematics. Common Core State Standards (College- and Career-Readiness Standards and K–12 Standards in English Language Arts and Math)*. Washington, D.C.: NGA Center and CCSSO, 2010. http://www.corestandards.org/.

Shumway, Jessica F. *Number Sense Routines: Building Numerical Literacy Every Day in Grades K–3*. Portland, Maine: Stenhouse Publishers, 2011.

Today's Number

A first-grade class is told that today's number is 15. The students think quietly for a bit and then begin to share what they know about 15.

Alex comments, "I know that 15 is 5 more than 10."

"The speed limit in front of the school is 15," adds Max.

Lucy shares, "If you count by 5s, you'll get to 15."

Down the hall, a class of fifth graders is thinking about ¾. The teacher asks students to talk with a partner and create a list of everything they know about ¾.
Partners Quintin and Carley's list includes the following:

- ¾ is a fraction.

- ¾ and 75% are equal.

- ¾ is more than ½.

In a seventh-grade classroom across town, students have been asked to suggest what they know about −8.

Brian states, "−8 is the opposite of 8."

His teacher asks him to explain his thinking.

"Well, −8 and 8 are on different sides of 0, but they are the same number of spaces away from zero. It's kind of like symmetry," Brian responds.

Implementing the Routine

The Today's Number routine involves presenting a carefully selected "number of the day" to students. The students then generate a variety of representations of the number, including drawings, equations, and examples. Generating and sharing these representations allows students to grow in the ways they think about numbers and operations.

The number of the day may be presented to students in various ways. In the early elementary grades, the teacher may present the problem orally to the entire class and create a group list of representations as the students orally share. Figure 1.1 shows some of the ways a kindergarten class thought about the number 7. In later grades, Today's Number may be posted, projected, or simply distributed as the students enter the room. Older students may first create a list individually or in small groups. Working in small groups creates a level of confidence that will encourage students to more willingly share their representations. As students work, the teacher has the opportunity to listen to their discussions, to look at the representations being created, and to carefully choose and sequence representations to be shared that are most apt to benefit students' understanding. The discussions that occur as students share their representations are a valuable part of the growth that results from implementing this routine.

Fig. 1.1.

Kindergarten class representations of 7

Maintaining an ongoing record of student responses to Today's Number is another important part of the routine. Class charts may be created and posted so that students have a record of their thinking about a variety of numbers. Such a practice will allow the teacher to observe growth in student thinking as the year progresses. In addition, the teacher could compile the work generated by students to create a class book of Today's Number. Students may also record their representations of various numbers of the day in individual notebooks or journals. This, too, will provide ongoing evidence of growth in how students think about numbers and operations.

Mathematical Content and Practices

The Today's Number routine is easily implemented but can yield powerful results both in mathematical content and in mathematical practices. One benefit of the use of this routine is the growth in number sense it promotes. Shumway (2011) describes students with a sense of number as demonstrating a sense of what numbers mean, an ability to look at the world in terms of quantity and numbers, an ability to make comparisons among quantities, flexibility and fluidity with numbers, and an ability to perform mental math. The development of number sense should be considered at all grade levels. Reys and colleagues (2012) suggest that the development of number sense is a lifelong process and not an innate ability that students either have or do not have. Thus, number sense should not be viewed as a unit to be covered but rather as a daily thread that runs through all the mathematics work undertaken by students. The whole-number sense developed at the elementary level extends to number sense related to fractions, decimals, percent, integers, exponents, and roots in middle school. Number sense is further extended as high school students gain understanding of the real number system. Although the actual numbers used as Today's Number will change across grade levels, the consistent use of this routine throughout the grades will continue to enhance number sense.

The implementation of Today's Number—careful selection of a number, generation and recording of representations of the number, observation and discussion of representations of others, and response to teacher questioning—provides a structured way to enhance number sense. Two aspects of number sense encouraged by the use of Today's Number are the composition and decomposition of numbers and the use of part–whole relationships. In addition, students will gain valuable experience in generating equivalent expressions and creating new numerical expressions by modifying expressions suggested previously.

The Today's Number routine also allows students to develop the eight mathematical practices described in the Common Core State Standards for Mathematics (National Governors Association Center for Best Practices and Council of Chief State School Officers 2010; see appendix A). One practice involves the construction of viable arguments and the critique of the reasoning of others. Explaining their thinking is not an easy task for students working at any level. In fact, many mathematically proficient and gifted students have a great deal of difficulty explaining how they arrived at an answer. The open-ended nature of the Today's Number task allows for responses at multiple levels of thinking and gives students the opportunity to explain their thinking. Students also have the opportunity to informally critique the justifications provided by others as they hear other students explain their own representations. Another mathematical practice enhanced by the use of Today's Number is making use of the structure of mathematics. Many students will provide representations of the number of the day that are based on the decomposition of the number. As they decompose a variety of numbers, patterns will emerge. For example, when thinking about the number 48, a student may first suggest that 48 could be presented as 6×8. Another student may use this fact to suggest thinking about 6×8 as $6 \times 5 + 6 \times 3$. Such representations suggested over time for a variety of numbers will result in a foundation for learning about the distributive property.

A variety of models may be used across grade levels with Today's Number, and the consistent use of these models will provide curricular articulation and coherence. Bar, part–whole, number bond, and number line models may each be used at any grade level. Bar, part–whole, and number bond models may be used to illustrate decomposition, and the number line model used to represent the comparison of the number of the day to other numbers. Figure 1.2 shows the use of these models for a variety of Today's Numbers. Teachers should look for and capitalize on student use of these models when selecting sample representations to be shared with the class. If these models are not suggested by students, the teacher may choose to introduce them as a way to represent Today's Number. In the student work we collected, students often used the number line model, but few used the other models without teacher prompting.

Assessing Student Thinking

Allowing students to share their representations and learn from each other is a vital component of Today's Number and provides the teacher with a great deal of information about how students are thinking about numbers. Some individual think time followed by the opportunity to share in small groups before sharing with the whole class will promote a classroom

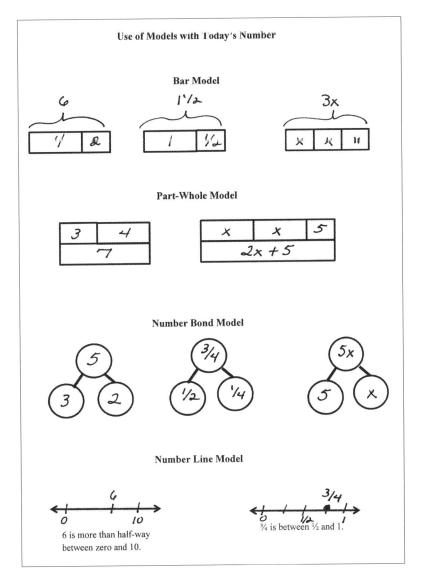

Fig. 1.2.
Use of models with Today's Number

environment that validates the importance of the thinking of all students and the importance of communication in mathematics. Shumway (2011) suggests that for teachers the difficult part of this routine is knowing what to look for in student work and how to highlight important math concepts as the students share their representations. She provides a list of common big ideas to look for in student work, including decomposing the number; using various groupings of ones, tens, hundreds, and thousands; using a pattern; looking at numbers in interesting ways; and using a variety of ways of thinking about numbers.

In examining student work collected across grade levels, we noticed four consistent types of representations being used by students:

1. Composing/decomposing
2. Representing relationships to other numbers
3. Representing mathematics in the world
4. Using models

Figures 1.3–1.6 show examples of each of these common representations at various grade levels. Although no type is more important than another, teachers should recognize and have students share examples of each type.

$$10+5=15 \qquad 1+14=15 \qquad 2+13=15$$
$$7+8=15 \qquad 4+11=15 \qquad 9+6=15$$

10 plus 5 is 15, 15 is a odd namber
20 take away 4 is 15, 15 one 10 and 5 ones

Fig. 1.3a and 1.3b.
Second graders use decomposition to represent 15.

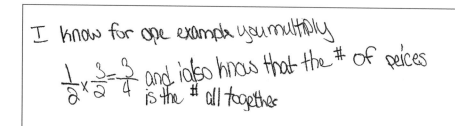

I know for one exampl you multiply
$\frac{1}{2} \times \frac{3}{2} = \frac{3}{4}$ and i also know that the # of peices
is the # all together

Fig. 1.3c.
A fifth grader represents ¾ by using decomposition.

5 is a hien number then 10.

1. 15 has 2 digers.
2. It is betwen 14 and 16.
3. you can get to 15 by counting by 5s.
4. 15 is bigger than 10.

Fig. 1.4a and 1.4b.

A first grader (top) and second grader (bottom) represent 15 by illustrating relationships to other numbers.

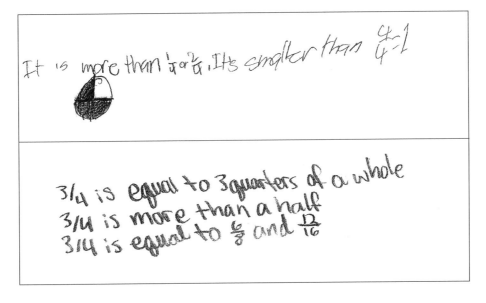

It is more than $\frac{1}{4}$ or $\frac{2}{4}$. Its smaller than $\frac{4}{4} - 1$

3/4 is equal to 3 quarters of a whole
3/4 is more than a half
3/4 is equal to $\frac{6}{8}$ and $\frac{12}{16}$

Fig. 1.4c and 1.4d.

A fourth grader (top) and fifth grader (bottom) show how ¾ is related to other numbers.

Adapting the Routine

The open-ended nature of this routine allows responses from students working at a variety of levels. However, when students are familiar with the routine, the cognitive demand of the task may be altered by adding constraints to responses generated by the students. These constraints may be based on the mathematical content being studied at that particular time. For example, students may be instructed to use only certain operations as they consider representations for Today's Number. They may be asked to share representations that include multiples of 5 and 10 or representations that illustrate the commutative property. Students could be instructed to provide representations of the number of the day that do not include numbers or to make representations that include exactly three numbers. For example, if the number of the day was 30 and students were instructed to not use numbers in their representations, a student might suggest "The number of days in April." If students were required to use exactly three numbers, $(8 + 2) \times 3$ would be an appropriate representation of 30. In addition, students may be required to use specific models or to avoid the use of a particular model.

Conclusion

Today's Number is a flexible, easily implemented mathematical routine that results in improved number sense and use of mathematical practices. The nature of the routine allows it to be used throughout the school year and across many grade levels, thus promoting coherence and articulation. Sharing representations encourages students' confidence, communication, and reflection on their own thinking as well as the thinking of others. As students share and discuss their representations of Today's Number, the teacher will gain valuable insight into how the students are thinking about numbers and guidance in planning future instruction.

References

National Governors Association Center for Best Practices (NGA Center) and Council of Chief State School Officers (CCSSO). *Common Core State Standards for Mathematics. Common Core State Standards (College- and Career-Readiness Standards and K–12 Standards in English Language Arts and Math)*. Washington, D.C.: NGA Center and CCSSO, 2010. http://www.corestandards.org/.

Reys, Robert, Mary M. Lindquist, Diana V. Lambdin, and Nancy L. Smith. *Helping Children Learn Mathematics*. 10th ed. Hoboken, N.J.: John Wiley & Sons, 2012.

Shumway, Jessica F. *Number Sense Routines: Building Numerical Literacy Every Day in Grades K–3*. Portland, Maine: Stenhouse Publishers, 2011.

2

Mystery Number

2nd grade

Alexis, a second grader, has chosen 51 as her mystery number. She reads four clues she has written to the other students in her group:

> "My number has two digits. The tens digit is four more than the ones digit. My number is between 50 and 60. What is my number?"

> Andy uses a hundred chart to find Alexis's mystery number. Lydia sketches a number line and locates 50 and 60. Lucas lists the numbers between 50 and 60 as a starting point.

4th grade

A fourth-grade class has been learning about factors and multiples. The teacher assigns each of them a mystery number and reminds them to write four clues to help their classmates guess the number. He asks students to use either the word *factor* or the word *multiple* in one of their clues.

> Jake reads his clues: "My number is a multiple of 6. My number has 6 factors. My number is less than 5 × 5. What is my number?"

> After thinking for a bit, Riley says, "I think you need another clue."

6th grade Sixth graders Connor and Mikayla are working together to write clues for the number ¾. Here are their clues:

- The product of the numerator and denominator is 12.
- It is not an improper fraction.
- The denominator is a multiple of 4.
- The fraction is greater than ½.

They are pleased with their clues and are anxious to share them with the rest of the class.

Implementing the Routine

During the implementation of the Mystery Number routine, students are given a variety of mystery numbers. The students work individually, in pairs, or in small groups to write a series of clues for the mystery number assigned. The number of clues to be written may be determined by the teacher or left up to the students writing the clues. These clues are presented to others in the class, who use them to determine the mystery number. The clues may be revealed together or one at a time; however, revealing the clues one at a time allows for discussion of what is learned from each clue. The creation, sharing, and use of these clues provides a wealth of experiences with a variety of mathematical ideas and promotes growth in the way students think about numbers. In addition, as students are challenged to think carefully about the clues written and the sequencing of the clues, their critical thinking and problem-solving skills are enhanced.

The Mystery Number routine may be implemented in a variety of ways. Teachers of early elementary students may choose to introduce the routine by using a set of previously written clues. The students would then work as a class to find the mystery number. As the year progresses, the teacher might choose to have the class work together to write clues for a given number. This approach will allow the teacher to talk with the students about the characteristics of a good sequence of clues. In upper elementary and middle school grades, the students may be provided different mystery numbers and challenged to create a set of clues that would provide enough information for another student to find the mystery number. These numbers may be assigned randomly or they may be carefully chosen and assigned to allow for differentiation by ability. The students may also be allowed to select their own Mystery Numbers. Older students may also be asked to analyze two different sets of clues for a particular mystery number to determine the advantages and disadvantages of each set. Working in small groups provides support to students as they use or develop clues. As students share their clues with others in the class, the teacher has the opportunity to look for increasing levels of sophistication in how the students are thinking about numbers. Figure 2.1 provides examples of student work that show various levels and styles of thinking.

Teacher questioning is an important part of implementing this routine. Questions that will enhance the reasoning and problem-solving abilities of students include asking students to determine whether a set of clues leads to only one number or whether multiple answers are possible, determining whether the clue set contains extra clues, and considering the sequencing of clues.

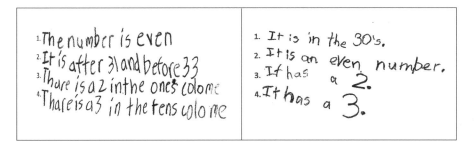

Fig. 2.1a1 and 2.1a2.
Although the clues for 32 written by these two students are similar, the student whose work is shown on the right understands that the clues should not be so specific that the answer is obvious.

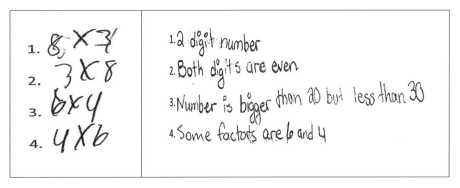

Fig. 2.1b1 and 2.1b2.
The fourth-grade student on the left wrote pairs of factors for 24; the other student planned clues more strategically. The third clue is essential to solving the problem. The clues on the right lead sequentially to the answer.

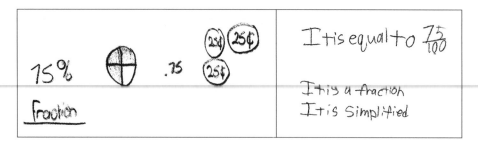

Fig. 2.1c1 and 2.1c2.
Two seventh-grade students approach the clue creation for 3/4 in different ways. The student on the left uses drawings. The student on the right creates the clues in such a way that all three are necessary to determine the answer.

Another important part of the Mystery Number routine is maintaining a record of student work on the routine. Students may create individual or class Math Riddle books that contain the clues written for a variety of Mystery Numbers. Additional riddles may be added to the book as the year progresses. The creation of these books will allow the teacher (and the students themselves) an opportunity to observe growth in student thinking throughout the year. This record of student work will also allow students to look at clues written earlier in the year and revise them. Sharing or exchanging books of these Mystery Numbers with other classes or creating Mystery Number books for younger children are additional ways to display work on this routine.

Mathematical Content and Practices

Mystery Number, an easily implemented routine, can result in positive growth in both mathematical content and mathematical practices. One benefit of the routine is the growth in number sense it promotes. Number sense is described by Howden (1989) as a "good intuition about numbers and their relationships. It develops gradually as a result of exploring numbers, visualizing them in a variety of contexts, and relating them in ways that are not limited by traditional algorithms" (p. 11). As students create clues for a mystery number and use clues to find a mystery number, they are exploring numbers and thinking of them in a variety of ways. The engaging nature of Mystery Number will encourage students of all ages, abilities, and interests to participate in the routine. Because Mystery Number may be used with whole numbers, fractions, percents, and integers, students at all grade levels may benefit from the use of the routine. Furthermore, consistent use of the routine will encourage number sense to continue to grow and supports the idea that the development of number sense is a lifelong process (Reys et al. 2012).

Many of the Standards for Mathematical Practice described in the Common Core State Standards for Mathematics (National Governors Association Center for Best Practices and Council of Chief State School Officers 2010; see appendix A) may be developed through the use of Mystery Number. These eight practices describe the processes and proficiencies that math teachers at all levels strive to develop in students. One of the eight practices describes mathematically proficient students as working to communicate precisely with others. The Mystery Number routine encourages this practice, as students carefully consider the clues they must give for another student to guess the number. Writing clues that lead to a single mystery number and sequencing the clues also promote precision in communication. In addition, as students participate in the Mystery Number routine, they attend to the meaning of quantities and create coherent representations of a problem—aspects of reasoning quantitatively. Finally, students must consider a logical progression of statements to be used as clues, and as the clues are shared with others, students may be called on to provide support for the clues they created. As they do so, they get experience constructing viable arguments.

Assessing Student Thinking

As students share the clues they create with others, the teacher has an opportunity to gain valuable information about how students are thinking about numbers, including looking for patterns in the clues students write and identifying misconceptions they may hold. Mystery Number is engaging and accessible to all students and, as a result, helps promote a classroom environment that supports the importance and value of all students' thinking.

In examining student work collected from several grade levels, we noticed some common types of clues being created by students:

- Use of relative magnitude or less than/greater than
- Use of mathematics vocabulary
- Use of unnecessary or redundant clues
- Use of computation to provide clues

Figures 2.2–2.5 show examples of these types of clues in student work from different grade levels.

1. The number is between 31 and 34. 2. The number is odd. 3. It has a 2 in the ones coalm. 4. It's less than 35.	It is greater than ½ It is less than 1 A multiple of it is 9/2 It is a fraction

Fig. 2.2a and 2.2b.

These students use the magnitude of numbers to provide clues for the mystery numbers 32 and ¾, respectively.

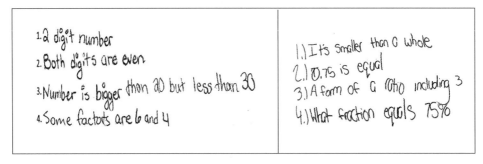

1. 2 digit number 2. Both digits are even 3. Number is bigger than 20 but less than 30 4. Some factors are 6 and 4	1.) It's smaller than a whole 2.) 0.75 is equal 3.) A form of a ratio including 3 4.) What fraction equals 75%

Fig. 2.3a and 2.3b.

Clues created by these students include mathematical vocabulary (factors, ratio) to provide clues for the mystery numbers 32 and ¾, respectively.

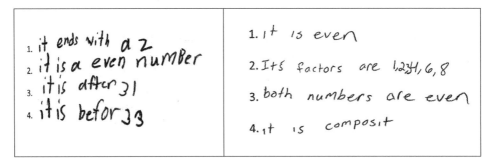

1. it ends with a 2 2. it is a even number 3. it is after 31 4. it is befor 33	1. it is even 2. Its factors are 1,2,4,6,8 3. both numbers are even 4. it is composit

Fig. 2.4a and 2.4b.

Many students included redundant clues. For example, the first two clues written by the student on the left give the same information. The student on the right wrote that the mystery number is composite, an unnecessary clue since the factors of the number had been listed earlier.

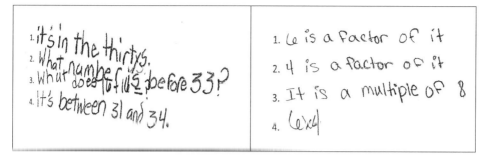

Fig. 2.5a and 2.5b.

These students asked readers to compute as one of the clues. The student on the left wrote 16 + 16, whereas the student on the right wrote 6 × 4.

Although Mystery Number is similar in some ways to the Today's Number routine described in chapter 1, the type of thinking required to generate clues that lead to a particular number is different from simply writing what is known about a number. The increased demand of writing clues for a mystery number is reflected in the student work we collected. This routine is often more challenging for students than Today's Number.

Adapting the Routine

Because this routine may be used with any number, it is accessible to students working at a variety of levels. The cognitive demand of the routine may be altered by adding some guidelines for the types of clues that must be included. These guidelines may be specific to the mathematical content currently being studied. For example, students may be instructed to use a particular term such as *factor* within their clue sets. Conversely, they may be instructed that they may not use a certain term or operation in the clues they create. They may be asked to create a set of clues that produces multiple possible answers or a set of clues that has some unnecessary clues included. Students may be instructed to include a model such as a number line as part of one of the clues they create. Finally, in the student work we collected, many students used relative magnitude for most or all of their clues (e.g., my number is larger than 24; my number is less than 5 × 6). Not allowing them to use clues such as these increases the cognitive demand and forces them to think of numbers in new ways. Mystery Number can be adapted to incorporate other mathematical content. For example, Mystery Number could become Mystery Shape as students write clues that lead their classmates to identify a secret shape or combination of shapes.

Conclusion

Mystery Number is easily implemented, and the use of this routine yields enhanced number sense and increased expertise with mathematical practices. The routine is almost endlessly adaptable to meet the needs of students working at various levels and at different grade levels. As students share their clues with others and respond to the clues of classmates, they are gaining valuable experience in communicating precisely and reasoning quantitatively. Teachers will gain insight into how their students are thinking about numbers as they listen to students share and work with clues leading to the mystery number.

References

Howden, Hilde. "Teaching Number Sense." *Arithmetic Teacher* 36 (February 1989): 6–11.

National Governors Association Center for Best Practices (NGA Center) and Council of Chief State School Officers (CCSSO). *Common Core State Standards for Mathematics. Common Core State Standards (College- and Career-Readiness Standards and K–12 Standards in English Language Arts and Math)*. Washington, D.C.: NGA Center and CCSSO, 2010. http://www.corestandards.org/.

Reys, Robert, Mary M. Lindquist, Diana V. Lambdin, and Nancy L. Smith. *Helping Children Learn Mathematics*. 10th ed. Hoboken, N.J.: John Wiley & Sons, 2012.

3

Alike and Different

1st
grade
In a first-grade classroom, the teacher writes the numbers 11 and 17 on the board. She asks the children to think about how the numbers are different and how they are alike. After a few minutes, she asks students to share what they thought. As they share, she creates a list of their responses on the board:

- Both are made with straight lines.

- Both are more than 10.

- Both have two digits.

- 17 is more than 11.

- The digits are the same for 11 but not for 17.

4th
grade
In the same school, the fourth-grade classes have been learning about fractions. At the beginning of class one day, the teacher asks Terry to suggest a fraction. Terry chooses 3/4. When Nancy is asked to suggest a fraction, she responds by selecting 5/8. The teacher asks the students to use their whiteboards to create a list of the ways 3/4 and 5/8 are alike and the ways they are different. Terry's list includes the following:

- Both are fractions.

- Both are less than 1.

- Both have odd numbers in the numerators.

- 3/4 is larger.

6th grade After working with fraction, decimal, and percent equivalencies, a sixth-grade teacher asks her students to work in pairs to create a list of the ways 0.62, ⁵/₈, and 61% are alike and the ways they differ. After a few minutes, she asks each pair to share their work with another pair. Trish, Cindy, Bob, and David list the following:

- All are greater than ¹/₂.

- They are not equal.

- They are all close to 60%.

- They are different representations.

- You could write all of them as fractions.

Implementing the Routine

The Alike and Different routine involves presenting students with two or more numbers, shapes, properties, and so forth. The students are then asked to think about and suggest ways in which the two are alike and the ways they are different. Silver (2010) suggests that such comparative thinking develops early and is important. He adds, "Without the ability to make comparisons—to set one object or idea against another and take note of similarities and differences—much of what we call learning would quite literally be impossible" (p. 6). In addition, Marzano, Pickering, and Pollock (2001) list identifying similarities and differences as one of the nine categories of instructional strategies proven to increase student achievement.

The Alike and Different routine may be implemented in a variety of manners depending on the needs of the students. The teacher may choose to preselect the items to be compared. For example, he or she may want to focus the students' thinking on the similarities and differences between prisms and pyramids. Careful selection of the numbers, shapes, properties, and so forth, to be compared allows the teacher to focus student thinking on the desired mathematical concept. Student choice could be incorporated by establishing some parameters, asking each student to choose and record two numbers, and then having each student exchange numbers with another student. In addition, the items to be compared could be drawn randomly from a box containing a variety of possibilities, or students could be asked to suggest items for all in the class to consider.

The benefit to be gained from this routine will be increased by allowing students some quiet, individual thinking and recording time before sharing with others. After this, the teacher may choose to have students share in pairs, in small groups, or as a class. Allowing students to hear how others thought about the numbers or shapes being considered and how they are alike and different will enhance the learning of all. Encouraging students to explain and justify their choices of how the items are alike and different will provide valuable experience in using reasoning to construct mathematical arguments. In addition, asking a student to explain the reasoning of another student emphasizes the importance of listening in the communication process.

Recording student responses by using a Venn diagram or other graphic organizer is helpful with this routine. Venn diagrams clearly indicate the similarities and differences of the two numbers, shapes, and so forth. Figure 3.1 shows Venn diagrams created by students completing the Alike and Different routine. The first diagram was used by a fifth grader thinking about 3/4 and 5/8, whereas the second was used by a seventh grader comparing 5/8 and 61%. (Interestingly, although most of the students had been exposed to Venn diagrams, in the work we collected, few students used a Venn diagram without teacher prompting.) Posting class diagrams or having students work in journals or individual notebooks will provide an ongoing record that allows the teacher to see growth in the sophistication of the students' thinking. This strategy will also enable children to look back at the ways they thought about particular numbers or shapes that they had considered previously.

Fig. 3.1.
Students use Venn diagrams to show how two numbers are alike and different.

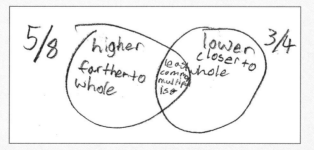

3.1a. A fifth-grade student organized his thinking about how 5/8 and 3/4 are alike and different by using a Venn diagram.

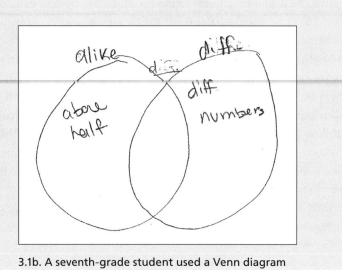

3.1b. A seventh-grade student used a Venn diagram to show how $5/8$ and 61% are alike and different, although the use of Alike and Different as the labels is unexpected.

Mathematical Content and Practices

The flexibility of the Alike and Different routine allows it to be used with a wide variety of mathematical content. Encouraging children to compare a variety of pairs of numbers will assist in the development of their number sense. The National Council of Teachers of Mathematics (2000), in its *Principles and Standards for School Mathematics,* suggests that instructional programs should equip children to understand numbers, ways of representing numbers, relationships among numbers, and number systems. As students consider pairs of numbers and how they are both alike and different, they will be gaining experience in identifying the relationships between numbers, and as a result, their understanding of numbers will increase. In addition, this routine may also be used for other mathematical ideas. For example, students may be asked to compare triangles and quadrilaterals, area and perimeter, mean and median, experimental and theoretical probability, rotations and reflections, or the commutative and associative properties. Because of the variety of mathematical content that may be used with this routine, it is very adaptable to many grade levels and abilities.

As students compare numbers, they will have the opportunity to develop the eight Standards for Mathematical Practice described in the Common Core State Standards for Mathematics (National Governors Association Center for Best Practices and Council of Chief State School Officers 2010; see appendix A). One of the standards, reason abstractly and quantitatively, includes the ability to create coherent representations of a problem, to attend to the meaning of the quantities involved, and to flexibly use different properties of operations and objects. As students identify similarities and differences between numbers and objects, they will gain valuable experience in each of these practices. A second Standard for Mathematical Practice describes mathematically proficient students as having the ability to construct viable arguments and critique the reasoning of others. The description of this standard states, "Students at all grades can listen or read the arguments of others, decide whether they make sense, and ask useful questions to clarify or improve the arguments" (p. 7). As students explain the characteristics they identified as being alike or different and listen to the reasoning of others, they will be moving toward meeting this standard.

Assessing Student Thinking

The time spent allowing students to share their work and as a result learn from each other is an important part of this routine. Asking students to share in pairs or small groups prior to a class discussion will provide time for the teacher to look for and sequence ideas to be presented during the class discussion. Sequencing so that simpler similarities and differences are shared first and the more sophisticated ideas are shared later in the discussion will ensure that all students have the opportunity to participate and learn. Figures 3.2 and 3.3 illustrate how students at two different grade levels thought about two numbers and the similarities and differences they noted. The work shown provides an example of how a teacher might choose to sequence the sharing of similarities and differences.

Fig. 3.2.

Second-grade student work for the task of describing how 29 and 50 are alike and different

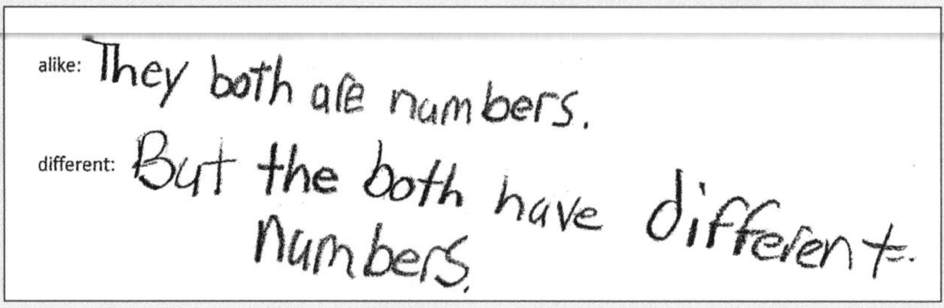

alike: They both are numbers.

different: But the both have different numbers.

3.2a. The obvious similarity and difference noted by this student would be a good starting point for class sharing.

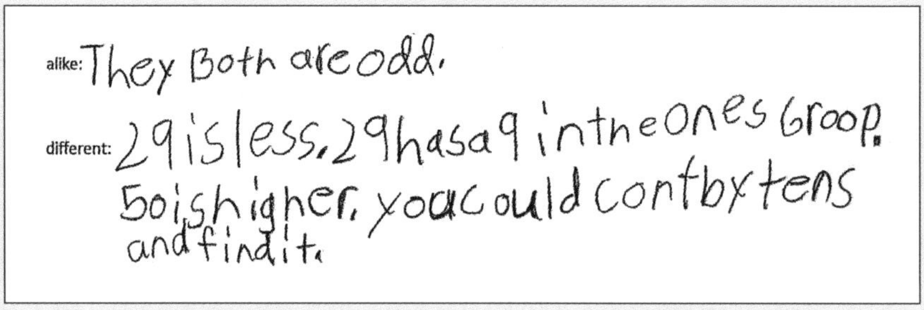

alike: They Both are odd.

different: 29 is less. 29 has a 9 in the ones Groop. 50 is higher. you ac ould cont by tens and find it.

3.2b. This student shares an incorrect likeness between the numbers. However, the differences noted are more specific than those in the above example.

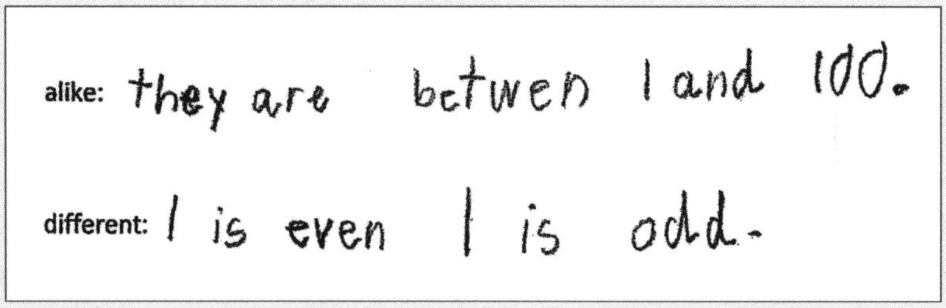

alike: they are betwen 1 and 100.

different: 1 is even 1 is odd.

3.2c. This student classifies the numbers as odd or even. An interesting follow-up question would be to ask the student how she knows whether a number is odd or even.

Fig. 3.3.
Fifth-grade student work for the task of describing how ³/₄ and ⁵/₈ are alike and different.

> ¹ They are both fractions!
>
> ² They have different numbers.

3.3a. The response given by this student contains an obvious similarity and difference and would best be shared early in the class discussion.

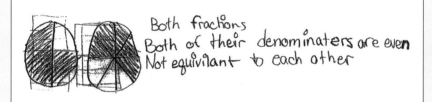

> Both fractions
> Both of their denominaters are even
> Not equivilant to each other

3.3b. A more detailed response is given by this student, who drew a picture to support the statement that the two fractions are not equivalent.

> They both cant be syplifyed, They are both fractions. The numtors are prime. The denomonators are even, The denomonators are composite

3.3c. This student identified only similarities but did notice several ways that the fractions were alike.

Adapting the Routine

Alike and Different is an open-ended task that allows responses from students working at any level. Students are free to suggest basic similarities or differences or much more sophisticated and less obvious ones. The level of cognitive demand of the task may be altered in a variety of ways. For example, the teacher may ask each student to suggest a specified number of similarities or differences. Choosing items to be compared when one item is a subset of the other also alters the demand of the task. For example, describing how triangles and quadrilaterals are alike and different is a much more straightforward task than describing the similarities and differences between squares and rectangles. Since squares are special rectangles and thus have the same properties, thinking about how to describe the difference between the two is interesting and challenging. Identifying specific terms to be included in the list of similarities and differences also changes the cognitive demand and allows the teacher to focus on particular mathematics content. For example, students might be asked to list how 24 and 36 are alike and different with the requirement that the terms *factor* and *multiple* be used. Depending on the terms specified, this may provide a level of support for students struggling with identifying similarities and differences. Alternatively, the required terms may be chosen to present a challenge as students compare the two items under consideration.

Conclusion

The Alike and Different routine is easily implemented and flexible, in that a wide variety of mathematical content may be incorporated. The routine may be used at any point during a lesson and is appropriate for use at any grade level. As students explain and justify their choices, they grow in mathematical content knowledge and the ability to reason and communicate about mathematical ideas.

References

Marzano, Robert J., Debra J. Pickering, and Jane E. Pollock. *Classroom Instruction That Works: Research-Based Strategies for Increasing Student Achievement.* Alexandria, Va.: Association for Supervision and Curriculum Development, 2001.

National Council of Teachers of Mathematics (NCTM). *Principles and Standards for School Mathematics.* Reston, Va.: NCTM, 2000.

National Governors Association Center for Best Practices (NGA Center) and Council of Chief State School Officers (CCSSO). *Common Core State Standards for Mathematics. Common Core State Standards (College- and Career-Readiness Standards and K–12 Standards in English Language Arts and Math).* Washington, D.C.: NGA Center and CCSSO, 2010. http://www.corestandards.org/.

Silver, Harvey F. *Compare and Contrast: Teaching Comparative Thinking to Strengthen Student Learning.* Alexandria, Va.: Association for Supervision and Curriculum Development, 2010.

Number Lines

1st grade First graders Kristen and Jagan are working together to locate 13 on a number line with only 10 and 20 marked.

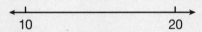

       10   20

Jagan quickly states that 13 is closer to 10 than to 20, so 13 should be marked "pretty close" to the 10 on the number line. Kristen agrees but pushes for a more precise location of 13. She says, "15 would be the middle, right? So 15 would be here." She draws a tick mark for 15. "Let's count backwards from here to see where 13 would be." Kristen draws two more tick marks for 14 and 13.

4th grade A fourth-grade class has been asked to determine the number being indicated by an arrow pointing to a number line.

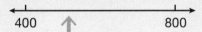

       400   800

Becca, Mahmoud, and Paul are discussing their thinking. Becca comments, "I think the arrow is at 500 because halfway between 400 and 800 is 600. The arrow is about halfway between 400 and where 600 is. So it's 500." Paul disagrees, "No, it's 410 because it is close to the 400 mark but not right on it." Mahmoud adds, "I think Becca is right. The arrow is about one-quarter of the way to 800."

6th grade During a preassessment, a sixth-grade teacher asks his students to determine where $3/5$ would be located on a number line with 0 and 1 marked. After giving them time to work individually, he collects their work. He notices many different responses and reasons given to support the responses. Some students divide the space between 0 and 1 and use this to help them locate $3/5$. Others convert $3/5$ to a decimal and use this to help determine the location of $3/5$. Several students use benchmark fractions such as $1/2$ and $3/4$ to help with locating $3/5$.

Implementing the Routine

The Number Line routine involves presenting students with a number line that may have only one or two values marked on it. The students are then asked to locate a particular value or determine the value of an indicated location and explain their thinking. The number line is a powerful, coherent, and unifying model that may be used across multiple grade levels to develop number sense and computational proficiency. In addition, the Common Core State Standards for Mathematics (National Governors Association Center for Best Practices and Council of Chief State School Officers 2010) refers often to the use of the number line. However, Frykholm (2010) comments, "One of the most overlooked tools of the elementary and middle school classroom is the number line. Typically displayed above the chalkboard right above the alphabet, the number line is often visible to children, though rarely used as effectively as it might be" (p. 5).

The Number Line routine is flexible and allows for a variety of implementation strategies. The teacher may choose to display a class number line and have all the students work on locating the same value. For example, a number line with 0 and 1 marked on it is displayed and all students are asked to locate $3/4$ and to be prepared to share their thinking. Allowing students to work in pairs or small groups to locate values may be beneficial in enhancing number sense, because children will then hear how others think about the magnitude of numbers. The teacher may also choose to give individuals or small groups different numbers, allowing the conversation to focus on relative magnitudes. This allows the teacher to differentiate based on the needs and abilities of the students in the class. Also, Bay (2001) suggests using a rope held at each end by students in the class to create a life-sized number line. Using a long rope or simply creating a large number line on a wall will allow students to more precisely locate values since smaller partitions may be used. Students may also be asked to establish two points on a number line, mark a location between those two points, and exchange number lines with another group. The group will then work together to determine the value of the marked location.

The Number Line routine may also be used with computation. For example, a student may be asked to use an empty number line to solve 42 − 29. An empty number line (a number line with no numbers or markers) is a tool that may enhance students' mental math skills and proficiency with operations. When using an empty number line, students mark only the numbers that are needed for their calculations (Bobis 2007). In so doing, their thinking strategies are revealed. Figure 4.1 shows three different methods of solving 42 − 29 by using empty number lines.

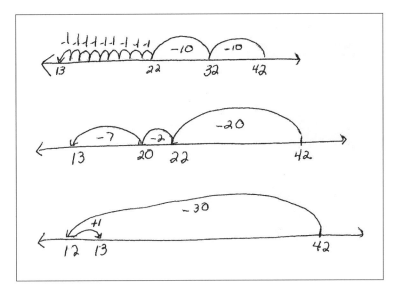

Fig. 4.1.

Three different student methods of solving 42 − 29 by using an empty number line

Bobis (2007) describes the link between an empty number line and the intuitive mental strategies children use as an advantage. She suggests that students will first focus on counting strategies and then, as they become more proficient, move to using combinations of counting strategies and partitioning strategies. The empty number line can also encourage the use of more sophisticated strategies as students record their computational strategies on the number line and share their thinking with others. This process also allows the teacher to see misconceptions and adjust instruction accordingly (Bobis 2007).

As with many mathematical routines, students will benefit from being allowed some individual time to think and record their thinking before sharing with others. Having students share the thinking process they used to determine the location of a value or the value of an indicated location will help develop the number sense of all students in the class. Also, in sharing their thinking with others, students will get practice in communicating mathematically.

Mathematical Content and Practices

The Number Line routine may be used at multiple grade levels to enhance number sense and computational proficiency. Students in the lower elementary grades use number lines to develop an understanding of the magnitude and order of whole numbers. Van de Walle, Karp, and Bay-Williams (2010) do caution that a number line can initially present conceptual difficulties for young students owing to the difficulty in seeing the unit when it appears on a continuous line. In addition, they suggest difficulty may arise because a number line marks a shift from counting a number of objects in a collection to units of length. They advise teachers to emphasize the unit (length) to avoid misconceptions arising from student focus on the hash marks instead of the spaces between them. Figure 4.2 shows examples of work from second graders.

Fig. 4.2.
Examples of second-grade work locating 13 on a number line

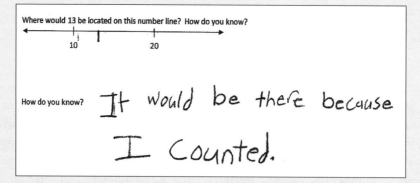

Where would 13 be located on this number line? How do you know?

10   20

How do you know? It would be there because I counted.

4.2a. This student marked and then erased tick marks to help with locating 13. The student then counted to locate 13 fairly accurately.

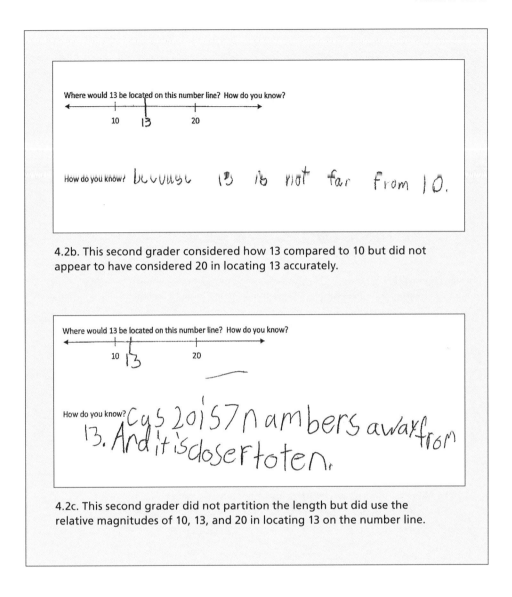

Where would 13 be located on this number line? How do you know?

10   13   20

How do you know? because 13 is not far from 10.

4.2b. This second grader considered how 13 compared to 10 but did not appear to have considered 20 in locating 13 accurately.

Where would 13 be located on this number line? How do you know?

10 13   20

How do you know? Cys 20 is 7 nambers away from 13. And it is closer to ten.

4.2c. This second grader did not partition the length but did use the relative magnitudes of 10, 13, and 20 in locating 13 on the number line.

As students move into upper elementary grades, the number line continues to be a valuable tool for number sense development. Varied levels of understanding and explanation are commonly seen in the work of students. Figure 4.3 shows the work of some fourth-grade students asked to determine the value marked by an arrow placed on a number line with 400 and 800 marked.

Fig. 4.3.

Four examples of fourth-grade work determining the value of a location marked on the number line

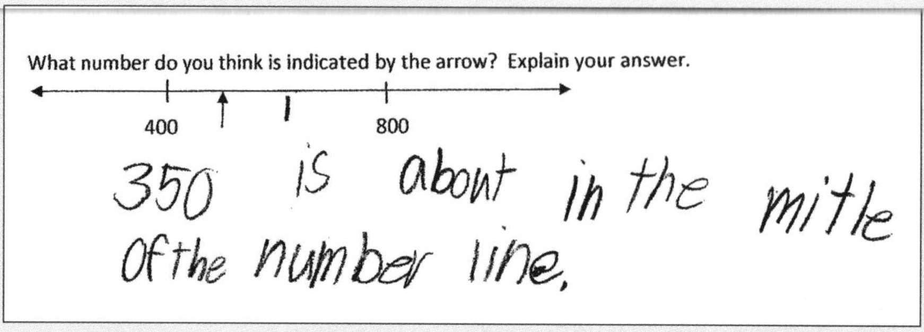

What number do you think is indicated by the arrow? Explain your answer.

400   800

350 is about in the mitle of the number line.

4.3a. This student marked and then erased tick marks to help with locating 13. The student then counted to locate 13 fairly accurately.

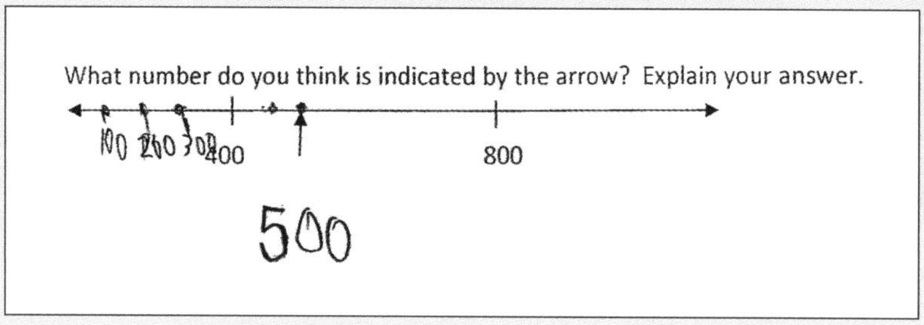

What number do you think is indicated by the arrow? Explain your answer.

100 200 300 400   800

500

4.3b. Interestingly, this student did not consider the 800 in determining the value of the arrow. Another interesting aspect of the work is that although the student made two tick marks after 400, he labeled the second 500.

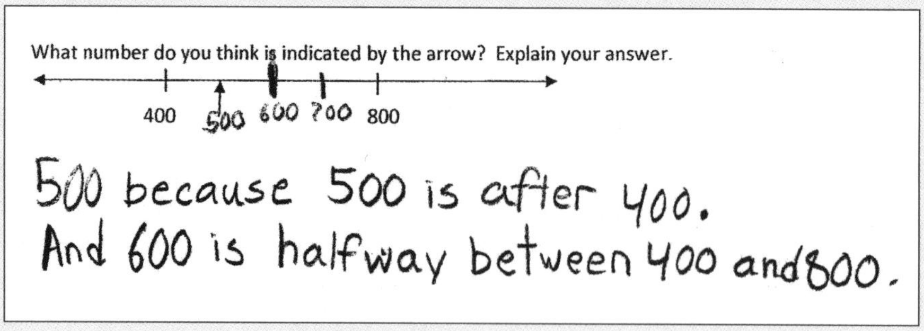

What number do you think is indicated by the arrow? Explain your answer.

400   500 600 700 800

500 because 500 is after 400.
And 600 is halfway between 400 and 800.

4.3c. The fourth-grade student's process results in a correct answer, but her explanation does not fully explain how she thought about the number line.

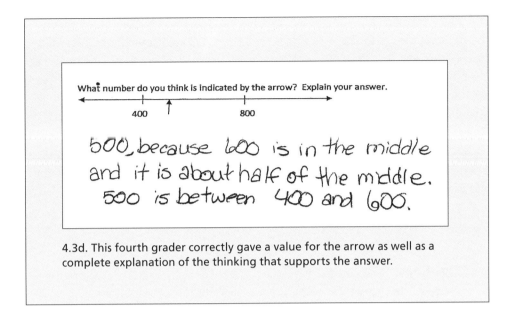

What number do you think is indicated by the arrow? Explain your answer.

400   800

500, because 600 is in the middle and it is about half of the middle. 500 is between 400 and 600.

4.3d. This fourth grader correctly gave a value for the arrow as well as a complete explanation of the thinking that supports the answer.

Bay (2001) suggests many uses for the number line in the upper grades. For example, the relative size of very large numbers can be explored using number lines. Students may be asked to locate 4,096 on a number line with 0 and 10,000 marked. Then the upper point is changed to 100,000 or 1,000,000, causing students to relocate 4,096.

Rounding numbers is difficult for many students, and the use of a number line may provide the visual representation needed to overcome this difficulty. The Number Line routine can be adapted to include problems asking students to use the number line to round. For example, suppose students are asked to round 578 to the nearest hundred. Marking 500 and 600 on the number line since 578 is between them, marking the halfway point of 550, and then marking 578 on the number line will help students realize that 578 is nearer 600 and thus rounds to 600 (see fig. 4.4).

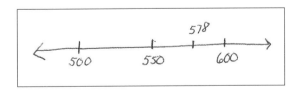

Fig. 4.4.
Use of a number line to assist in rounding

The Common Core State Standards for Mathematics (National Governors Association Center for Best Practices [NGA Center] and Council of Chief State School Officers [CCSSO] 2010) calls for students in third grade to understand a fraction as a number on the number line and to represent fractions on a number line diagram. Reys and colleagues (2012) emphasize the need for students to have many prior experiences with number lines before being asked to understand the number line as a model for fractions. The difficulties students have in locating rational numbers on a number line are illustrated in figure 4.5, which shows the responses of some fifth graders asked to locate 3/5 on a number line and explain their thinking.

Fig. 4.5.

Fifth-grade students locate 3/5 on a number line and explain their thinking.

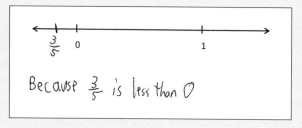

4.5a. This student mistakenly believes that fractions are less than 0.

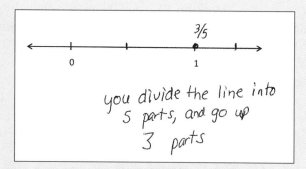

4.5b. The student does not understand the whole as a unit of length and instead partitions the entire line into fifths.

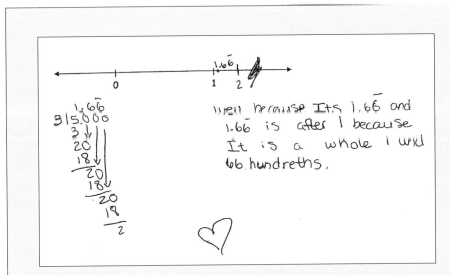

4.5c. This student understands that fractions and decimals are related but fails to see that an error in computation produces an unreasonable answer.

The use of the Number Line routine with rational numbers helps overcome the difficulty students face in using the number line model. Teachers will want to consider marking the number line with negatives and with numbers greater than 1 to allow for the development and discussion of misconceptions regarding the location of rational numbers on the number line.

An interesting use of the number line to develop algebraic reasoning is suggested by Bay (2001). She suggests the use of the number line to explore algebraic expressions. The number 0 is placed on the number line and then the variable x is placed arbitrarily on the line, allowing the students to know whether x represents a positive or negative value. Students are asked to determine the location of expressions such as $3x$, x^2, $x + 2$, and $x - 5$. After placing the expressions on the number line, the students are asked to consider whether the placement is possible and whether the location marked is the only place the value could be located.

As students locate values on the number line and find the value of specified locations, they can use and develop many of the eight Standards for Mathematical Practice described in the Common Core State Standards for Mathematics (see appendix A). By using the Number Line routine, students come to see the number line as a useful tool and can use it strategically and appropriately to solve problems. Using the number line assists them in reasoning quantitatively and requires them to use precision with the number line as well as in communicating their thinking about the number line. Finally, as students explain their thinking to others, they are gaining experience in constructing viable arguments while learning to listen and critique the reasoning of others.

Assessing Student Thinking

Allowing students time to share their work with the Number Line routine is an important part of the routine. As teachers observe students working together and sharing their thinking, teachers will gain beneficial insight into the misconceptions students may have regarding the magnitude of numbers or about number lines. Some of these misconceptions are illustrated in the student work shown in figure 4.6.

Fig. 4.6.

Student work illustrating some misconceptions students hold

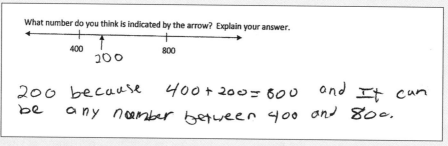

4.6a. A fourth-grade student has the misconception that a point on a number line can be labeled with any value as long as the value is between the indicated endpoints.

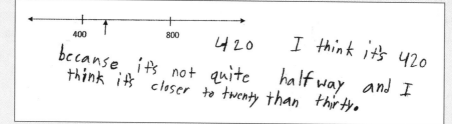

4.6b. This fourth grader fails to consider the magnitude of the marked 800 in describing "halfway."

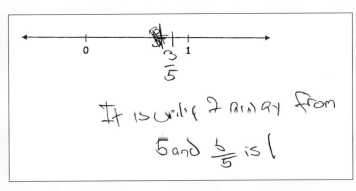

4.6c. The explanation offered by this fifth grader indicates that she does not understand the use of the denominator in locating a fraction on a number line.

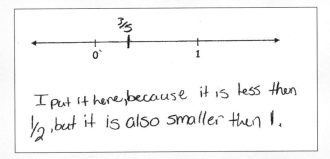

4.6d. A lack of understanding of the magnitude of fractions is shown in the work of this fifth-grade student.

Knowledge of these misconceptions will allow the teacher to modify instruction to address the misconceptions. Probing to better understand misconceptions is necessary. For example, the work in figure 4.7 might indicate that a student does not understand where 13 is located in comparison to 10 and 20. However, in reading the student's explanation that 13 is closer to 10 than to 20, the teacher will realize that the student does in fact understand the relative magnitudes of the number but is not connecting that knowledge to the visual representation of the number line.

When using an empty number line with computation, a careful selection of the student work to be shared with the class will encourage students to grow in computational proficiency. As students work, the teacher has the opportunity to select examples of more sophisticated thinking. For example, teachers may look for students who are successfully counting by tens from any starting value. They may also look for students who are successfully bridging tens in their work. To solve 9 + 4, the student partitions 4 into 1 + 3. The student adds in part: (9 + 1) + 3 = 13 (Bobis 2007).

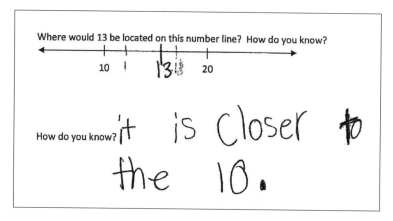

Fig. 4.7.
The student understands the relative magnitude of the numbers but cannot accurately represent this on the number line.

Adapting the Routine

The Number Line routine may be adapted so that students working at any level respond successfully. The numbers to be located or the points provided may be varied to alter the demand of the task. For example, if students are asked to locate 3/5 on a number line, marking 0, 1, and 2 increases the difficulty of the task. If students are being asked to determine the value of a location marked between 200 and 300, moving the location closer to the halfway mark may make the task more accessible to some students. If the empty number line is being used as a tool for computation, providing a variety of problems will allow for differentiation. For example, 45 + 23 is less demanding than 45 + 26 because of the need to bridge tens in the second example.

Conclusion

The Number Line routine is easily implemented and quite flexible in the mathematical content and level of demand that may be incorporated. Because of the flexibility of the routine, it may be used with students at any grade level. The number line is an important mathematical tool, and the use of this routine provides valuable experience in the use of the tool. Also, the frequent use of the number line in the elementary grades will help ease the transition to thinking about fractions on the number line. The routine encourages students to present viable mathematical arguments, attend to precision in mathematical communication, and become more proficient with quantitative reasoning.

References

Bay, Jennifer. "Developing Number Sense on the Number Line." *Mathematics Teaching in the Middle School* 6 (April 2001): 448–51.

Bobis, Janette. "The Empty Number Line: A Useful Tool or Just Another Procedure?" *Teaching Children Mathematics* 13 (April 2007): 410–13.

Frykholm, Jeffrey. *Learning to Think Mathematically with the Number Line, K–5.* Boulder, Colo.: Cloudbreak Publishing, 2010.

National Governors Association Center for Best Practices (NGA Center) and Council of Chief State School Officers (CCSSO). *Common Core State Standards for Mathematics. Common Core State Standards (College- and Career-Readiness Standards and K–12 Standards in English Language Arts and Math).* Washington, D.C.: NGA Center and CCSSO, 2010. http://www.corestandards.org/.

Reys, Robert E., Mary M. Lindquist, Diana V. Lambdin, and Nancy L. Smith. *Helping Children Learn Mathematics.* 10th ed. Hoboken, N.J.: Wiley and Sons, 2012.

Van de Walle, John A., Karen S. Karp, and Jennifer M. Bay-Williams. *Elementary and Middle School Mathematics: Teaching Developmentally.* Boston: Pearson, 2010.

Quick Images

1st
grade

A first-grade teacher shows this dot arrangement to her students for a few seconds. The students are then asked to tell how many dots they saw and how they knew.

Ashley says, "There are four dots on the top row and three dots on the bottom row. Four and three more is seven." "I saw two dots going up and down. There's three of those and then one extra," adds Derrick. Bradley comments, "I kind of thought that, too, but I see six and then one sticking out."

3rd
grade

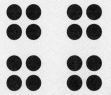

A similar exercise is taking place down the hall in a third-grade classroom. When asked to determine how many dots are in the arrangement above, students offer several different explanations.

Kayla notices there are four sets of four dots and concludes there are 16 dots in all since 4 × 4 = 16.

Julius also concludes there are 16 dots but explains that he saw four dots in each group and 4 + 4 = 8 for the top part of the arrangement. Since the bottom part is the same as the top, there are 16 dots since 8 + 8 = 16.

6th
grade

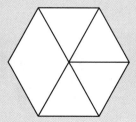

A sixth-grade teacher shows her class the figure above for a brief time. She then asks them to draw what they saw and to explain how they saw it.

Kieran writes, "I saw a rhombus with four triangles connected to it." Cooper's explanation differs. He describes what he saw as a hexagon divided into pieces with one of the pieces being bigger than the others. "I saw a three-dimensional cube," writes Samantha. Zach comments that he saw a hexagon with triangles inside it.

Implementing the Routine

When implementing the Quick Images routine, the teacher projects or holds up an image. The image may be an arrangement of dots, ten-frames, geometric figures, and so forth. After seeing the image for a very brief period, students are asked to tell the quantity shown or to draw or build a copy of what they saw. In addition, they are asked to explain *how* they saw the image. The teacher may choose to show the image for a second time to allow students an opportunity to revise and refine their mental image.

The ability to instantly see how many are in a small group is an example of the use of subitizing (Reys et al. 2012). Reys and colleagues provide several reasons why the ability to subitize is important. First, recognizing the quantity in a small group saves time because it is faster than counting each member in the group. Second, subitizing is a forerunner of powerful ideas related to number. For example, children who subitize demonstrate the knowledge of order relationships (4 is more than 2, and 4 is one less than 5). A third important aspect of subitizing is that it helps children develop more sophisticated counting techniques such as counting on. Finally, the ability to subitize assists with developing proficiency with addition and subtraction since students will not have to count but can instead focus on the action of the operation (Reys et al. 2012). Clements and Sarama (2009) state that subitizing starts developing very early and, when developed well, provides a foundation for mathematics through elementary, middle school, high school, and beyond.

Clements (1999) describes two types of subitizing. First, perceptual subitizing is the ability to perceive a quantity intuitively. This type of subitizing is demonstrated with small numbers. The second type of subitizing, conceptual subitizing, is the ability to see parts and put them together to create the whole. The explanations shown in the student work in figure 5.1 are examples of conceptual subitizing.

Fig. 5.1a1 and 5.1a2.
First-grade students explain how they saw this arrangement.

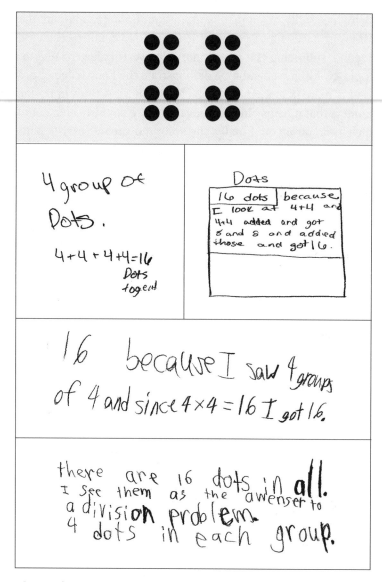

Fig. 5.1b1, 5.1b2, 5.1b3, 5.1b4.
Fourth-grade students describe how they saw this arrangement.

The Quick Images routine may be differentiated in many ways. Shumway (2011) suggests the use of several models, including dot cards, domino patterns, pictures, and dice patterns for subitizing. She comments that this variety of experiences will encourage children to think flexibly and will give the teacher knowledge of the depth of student understanding. Clements and Sarama (2009) provide a list of variations on the Quick Images routine:

- Ask students to use manipulatives to re create what they saw.

- Show several cards that all but one show the same number. Children are to determine which card does not match.

- Have children play a memory game with a rule in place that allows only a very short glimpse of what is turned over.

- Have children spread out a set of cards with 0 to 10 dots shown. Call a number and the child is to quickly pick up the card that matches.

- Ask students to name the number that is one or two more or less than the number shown on the Quick Image. (p. 11)

Asking students to explain how they "saw" the arrangement and knew the quantity or how they saw an arrangement of geometric shapes is an important part of the Quick Images routine. As students listen to explanations of others' thinking regarding Quick Images, they will "build a stronger visual understanding of amounts and relationships among numbers" (Shumway 2011, p. 42). Recording the thinking of students is also important. Teachers may choose to display arrangements on class charts and record all the ways students saw the arrangement. Such a practice will encourage growth in the ways students think about quantities.

Mathematical Content and Practices

The use of the Quick Images routine with number arrangements promotes a foundation for the development of number sense. As described above, the ability to subitize assists students in developing sophisticated counting techniques and with the development of addition and subtraction. In later grades, Quick Images may be used to help students visualize multiplicative ideas (Shumway 2011). For example, as seen in the third-grade vignette at the beginning of this chapter, students could be shown four groups of four dots to encourage them to see this as 4 × 4, or 16, dots. As students perform the Quick Images routine, they will have the opportunity to advance their mental math skills as they become more efficient and automatic with quantities (Shumway 2011). Showing students arrangements that are too large to subitize will provide practice with estimation. Quick Images could also be collections of base-ten blocks with the blocks being ungrouped by place value (see fig. 5.2). As the image is shown, students would need to mentally collect the place-value pieces to find the value.

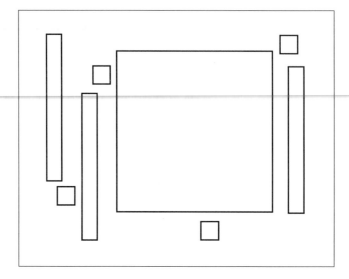

Fig. 5.2.
Arrangement of base-ten blocks not grouped by place
values

Quick Images can also be used to enhance the spatial skills of students. Students can be shown arrangements of geometric shapes for a short time and then be asked to draw what they saw. Having students write explanations about how they saw the arrangement provides a great deal of information about how students are thinking about geometric figures. As a variation, students could be asked to provide a set of directions verbally to another student so that the second student can re-create the drawing.

The Common Core State Standards for Mathematics (National Governors Association Center for Best Practices and Council of Chief State School Officers 2010) describes eight mathematical practices that educators should strive to develop in all students (see the complete text of all the practices in appendix A). The Quick Images routine allows students the opportunity to use structure, one of the practices, as they think about and describe how they saw a Quick Image. An example of the use of structure is found in the explanation provided by a student who sees the image shown in figure 5.3 and states that there are seven dots because there are three groups of two and one more. A pair of students may realize that although one of them sees four dots and three more while the other one sees three dots and four more, they will both see seven dots all together. This visual example of the commutative property is another example of the use of structure.

Fig 5 3
Dot arrangement shown to students

If students are asked to write an addition sentence to represent the Quick Image they saw, the mathematical practice of modeling with mathematics is being used. Finally, if students are asked to communicate what they saw, they must attend to precision. For example, suppose the arrangement in figure 5.4 is shown to one student and he or she is asked to describe the arrangement so that a second student could reproduce it. If precise communication is not used, the task will be quite difficult for the second student.

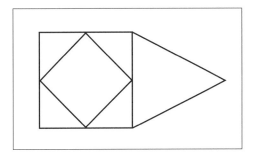

Fig. 5.4.
Geometric arrangement shown to students

Assessing Student Thinking

The use of the Quick Images routine and the student explanations that are part of the routine provide a great deal of information about how students are thinking about quantities. Listening to how students "saw" a quantity will provide insight into the number sense and mental mathematics of the students. The teacher will also see examples of the development of flexibility in working with quantities. When arrangements of geometric drawings are used for Quick Images, the vocabulary used provides information regarding the students' understanding of geometric concepts. The examples shown in figure 5.6 show the variety of ways students saw the geometric arrangement shown in figure 5.5.

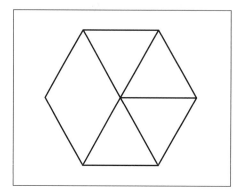

Fig. 5.5.

Geometric arrangement shown to students

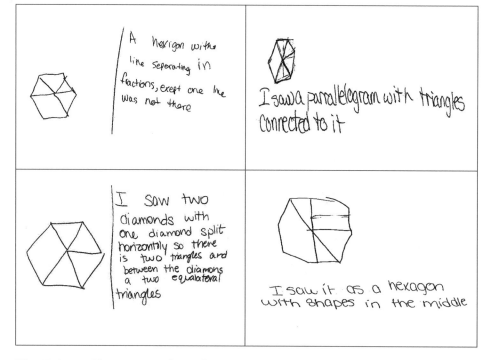

Fig. 5.6a, 5.6b, 5.6c, and 5.6d.

Seventh-grade students describe how they saw the geometric arrangement in figure 5.5.

Shumway (2011) provides an extensive list of questions that teachers may use to assess students' thinking. These questions include the following:

- How many did you see?
- How did you know it so quickly?
- Did you need to count?
- Did you count each dot, or did you just see the amount?
- How did you combine the dots to know how many? (p. 22)

Adapting the Routine

The Quick Images routine may be adapted by varying the images used. Starting with arrangements of very small quantities will provide practice with perceptual subitizing, whereas arrangements of larger values will encourage the use of conceptual subitizing. The use of Quick Images may be extended into upper grade levels as well. For example, students could be shown an image like the one in figure 5.7 and asked to provide the ratio of shaded to unshaded circles.

Fig. 5.7.
Example of image to be used with upper grade levels

Conclusion

The Quick Images routine is easy to implement while providing opportunities for students to develop and improve foundational mathematical concepts and skills. Because of the routine's flexibility, it may be used with students at a variety of grade levels and for a variety of purposes. Number sense and flexibility with addition and subtraction are two important areas of mathematics enhanced with the use of Quick Images. In addition, the routine provides valuable experience in attending to precision, modeling with mathematics, and using the structure of mathematics.

References

Clements, Douglas. H. "Subitizing: What Is It? Why Teach It?" *Teaching Children Mathematics* 5 (March 1999): 400–05.

Clements, Douglas H., and Julie Sarama. *Learning and Teaching Early Math: The Learning Trajectories Approach.* New York: Routledge, 2009.

National Governors Association Center for Best Practices (NGA Center) and Council of Chief State School Officers (CCSSO). *Common Core State Standards for Mathematics. Common Core State Standards (College- and Career-Readiness Standards and K–12 Standards in English Language Arts and Math).* Washington, D.C.: NGA Center and CCSSO, 2010. http://www.corestandards.org/.

Reys, Robert E., Mary M. Lindquist, Diana V. Lambdin, and Nancy L. Smith. *Helping Children Learn Mathematics.* 10th ed. Hoboken, N.J.: Wiley and Sons, 2012.

Shumway, Jessica F. *Number Sense Routines: Building Numerical Literacy Every Day in Grades K–3.* Portland, Maine: Stenhouse Publishers, 2011.

6

Guess My Rule

2nd grade A second-grade teacher shows her students a function machine with the rule "Subtract 6" written on it. She asks the students to create a list of "in" numbers and "out" numbers.

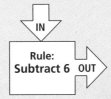

Ethan and Julius use a small whiteboard to begin recording their number pairs. Ethan suggests 10 as an in number with 4 as the out number. Julius says, "Let's put a 5 in. What would the out number be?" Ethan questions, "Will it work?"

3rd grade Third graders Joe and Andi are working together to find the rule being used to create the "in" and "out" numbers shown in the table below.

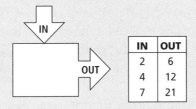

IN	OUT
2	6
4	12
7	21

Joe says, "The rule is to add 4 because 2 + 4 = 6." Andi responds, "That won't work, Joe, because 4 + 4 doesn't equal 12." "Is there more than one rule?" wonders Joe.

6th grade Jamie, a sixth grader, carefully unfolds the piece of paper her teacher had just given her. She reads, "Multiply by five, and add 2." Jamie and her partner Sam are playing a game of Guess My Rule. Sam's task is to guess the rule Jamie is holding. Sam suggests 2 as an input number. Jamie thinks for a minute and then tells Sam that the output number is 12. Sam says, "I know! The rule is multiply by 6!" After Jamie tells him this is not the correct rule, he suggests 5 as an input number. Jamie responds, "The output number would be 27." Sam says, "I'm not sure what the rule would be, but it has to have multiplication because the outputs are so much bigger than the inputs."

Implementing the Routine

Guess My Rule is a routine that involves having students analyze a set of number pairs to determine the rule that describes the relationship between them. The routine may also be implemented in a way that asks students to work from a given rule to generate a set of "in" and "out" numbers that would be created from the rule. This flexible, easily implemented routine provides the opportunity for students to develop algebraic thinking as they look for relationships among quantities. Soares, Blanton, and Kaput (2006) describe algebraic thinking as "a process in which students build general mathematical relationships and express these relationships in increasingly sophisticated ways" (p. 228). The Guess My Rule routine will encourage this thinking and representation of relationships.

Guess My Rule can be implemented in a variety of ways. Function machines can be used with the Guess My Rule routine. Function machines have a place for numbers to be input and a place for the result to be output. Within the "machine," a rule tells the machine what mathematical operations to perform on the input number to obtain the output number. Using a physical model of a function machine and a bit of drama on the part of the teacher increases the enjoyment students get from the routine. Reeves (2006) describes a first-grade teacher who created a function machine with a box large enough for students to physically get inside. She introduced the machine to her students by having a helper add pencils to the number of pencils input. In addition, students could be asked to create their own physical models for a function machine. Drawings of a function machine could also be created and laminated so that a variety of Guess My Rule games could be played.

Students may be provided the rule and then asked to determine the output generated for a given input. In addition, they may also be given a set of inputs and outputs and asked to determine the rule that describes the relationship between these. Older students can be asked to create their own rules for Guess My Rule. Each of these methods of implementation provides students valuable experience with algebraic thinking.

Recording the work of students provides ongoing assessment for teachers. Students may record Guess My Rule problems in individual journals so that they may look back at previously worked problems for guidance on new ones. Whole-group work on Guess My Rule could be recorded on large charts and displayed for quick reference by students. Asking students to explain their solution strategies and thinking in written form is also a valuable practice.

Regardless of how the routine is implemented, an important part of the routine is allowing time for students to verbally describe how they thought about the relationship among the quantities to solve the task presented. Students could be asked to work on the problem individually, work with a partner, or participate in a whole-class discussion about Guess My Rule. The time spent having students explain their thinking and approaches to a problem will result in the enhanced algebraic thinking of students and an improved ability to make mathematical arguments.

Mathematical Content and Practices

The Guess My Rule routine can be used at many different grade levels to engage students and enhance algebraic thinking. It is a good way to introduce young students to the idea of functions. In the simplest terms, a function is a relationship. More specifically, a function is a rule that uniquely defines how change in one variable affects change in the second variable (Van de Walle and Lovin 2006). Functions are one of the most important and powerful tools in mathematics because they allow the symbolic, visual, and verbal representation of relationships between variables (Van de Walle and Lovin 2006). Working with Guess My Rule will lay the foundation for a more formal study of functions in eighth grade and high school as described in the Common Core State Standards for Mathematics (National Governors Association Center for Best Practices and Council of Chief State School Officers 2010).

Varying the operations in rules gives students computational practice. Rules that include fractions or decimals allows students to practice computation with rational numbers in a fun way. Also, as they complete the routine, students gain

57

experience in using a variety of problem-solving strategies, including looking for a pattern and working backwards.

When students are allowed to choose the values to be used as input values, an interesting benefit occurs. When we as teachers choose the numbers to be used as input values, we often tend to select nice numbers. For example, if the rule is "divide by 2," we may hesitate to have the students use odd numbers. The unpredictability that results when students select the input values causes them to confront and deal with messy computation.

Several of the eight mathematical practices described in the Common Core State Standards for Mathematics (National Governors Association Center for Best Practices and Council of Chief State School Officers 2010; see appendix A) are developed through the Guess My Rule routine. For example, one calls for students to reason quantitatively and to consider relationships among quantities. As students work to determine the rule being used, they will be using this mathematical practice. Another mathematical practice, making viable mathematical arguments and critiquing the reasoning of others, can be enhanced if students are asked to explain and justify their thinking about Guess My Rule to others. Finally, using function machines, tables, verbal descriptions, and symbolic rules gives students the opportunity to model with mathematics, a third mathematical practice.

Assessing Student Thinking

Watching students complete the Guess My Rule routine and looking at the work they produce during the routine provides a great deal of insight into how students' algebraic thinking is developing. In looking at the student work we collected, we noticed some patterns in the responses of the students:

- Considering only one input–output pair in determining the rule
- Thinking that a pattern must exist in the numbers being input
- Expressing rules both symbolically and verbally

Some work indicated that the student considered only the first input–output pair when determining the rule being used. This occurred not only when the rule was provided and students were asked to generate pairs that fit the rule but also when students were to determine the rule. Figure 6.1 shows the work of a second-grade student asked to find pairs of numbers that would work in a function machine with a rule of "Add 2." This student correctly found that an input of 2 results in an output of 4. However, the student then looked at this first pair, noticed the 2 was doubled to get 4, and applied this doubling rule to the other pairs created. A fourth-grade student (see fig. 6.2) looked only at an input of 2 resulting in an output of 6 to suggest that the rule was "count by 4." The student did not pay attention to the other pairs in the table.

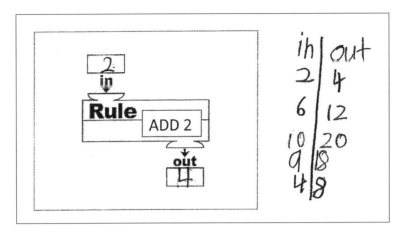

Fig. 6.1.
A second-grade student incorrectly applies the rule "Add 2."

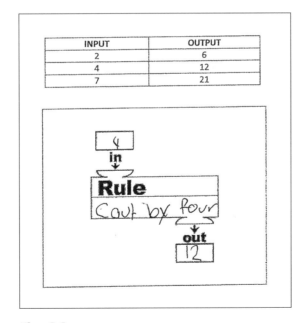

Fig. 6.2.
A fourth grader uses only the first pair of values to write a rule.

An interesting trend we noticed was that many students looked for a pattern in the numbers that were chosen as input values. For example, the two students whose work is shown in figures 6.3 and 6.4 each increased the number in the input column by one more than the increase in the previous pair. The student whose work is shown in figure 6.3 even indicates this pattern in what he recorded on the function machine. The work in figure 6.4 shows that this student also tried to find an additive pattern in the output numbers. An error in computation led the student to generate incorrect output values even though the correct rule was noted.

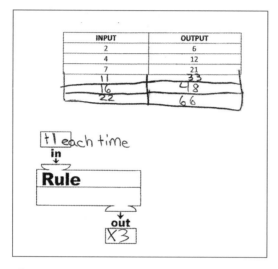

Fig. 6.3.
A fourth grader writes a rule for the function machine.

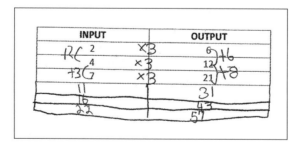

Fig. 6.4.
Another fourth grader works on the function machine problem.

Finally, many of the students simply recorded the rule on the function machine. However, some students chose to express the rule in writing (fig. 6.5). A few students were able to record the rule in a symbolic manner (fig. 6.6).

INPUT	OUTPUT
2	6
4	12
7	21

You take the input x 3 to get your output.

Fig. 6.5.
A fourth-grade student expresses the rule in writing.

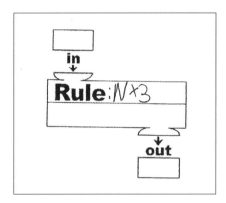

Fig. 6.6.
A fourth-grade student expresses the rule symbolically.

Adapting the Routine

The Guess My Rule routine may be adapted to allow students working at any level to participate. For example, a variety of rules could be provided within a single classroom. Students who need a challenge could work with rules that involve more than one operation, whereas those needing more support could work with single-operation rules. Decimals and fractions could be included in the rules for students needing to work on computation with rational numbers. The routine could be made more complex by providing inputs in one form and requiring outputs in another. For example, inputs could be in fraction form, and as part of the rule, outputs must be expressed as decimals. Varying the information provided to the students will also alter the demand of the task. Students can be given the input and rule and asked to find the output, they may be provided the rule and output and asked to find the input, or they may be provided the input and output and asked to find the rule. With very young children, sorting rules can be used with the Guess My Rule routine. Attribute blocks or other materials can be placed in Venn diagrams according to a secret rule. When the child believes he knows the rule, he can check his rule by placing a block in the diagram. After the teacher indicates whether the placement is correct, other students may take turns placing blocks to check the rules they notice.

Conclusion

The flexibility and easy implementation of the Guess My Rule routine makes it adaptable to students at any grade level. The mathematical content can be varied, as can the way the routine is implemented. Guess My Rule provides an introduction to the concept of functions, an important mathematical idea. The routine encourages students to reasons quantitatively, present viable mathematical arguments and critique the reasoning of others, and model with mathematics.

References

National Governors Association Center for Best Practices (NGA Center) and Council of Chief State School Officers (CCSSO). *Common Core State Standards for Mathematics. Common Core State Standards (College- and Career-Readiness Standards and K–12 Standards in English Language Arts and Math)*. Washington, D.C.: NGA Center and CCSSO, 2010. http://www.corestandards.org/.

Reeves, Charles A. "Putting Fun into Functions." *Teaching Children Mathematics* 12 (January 2006): 250–59.

Soares, June, Maria L. Blanton, and James J. Kaput. "Thinking Algebraically across the Elementary School Curriculum." *Teaching Children Mathematics* 12 (January 2006): 228–35.

Van de Walle, John A., and LouAnn H. Lovin. *Teaching Student-Centered Mathematics, Grades 5–8*. Boston: Pearson Education, 2006.

7

How Do You Know?

2nd grade
A second-grade teacher poses the following question to her students:

"How do you know that 12 is an even number?"

The students think quietly for a minute. Then each turns knee to knee with another student and begins talking.

Michelle tells her partner, Clinton, "It ends with a 2, so it's an even number because 2 is an even number." Clinton replies, "I know it's even because if you count by 2s you say 12 and you say all even numbers when you count by 2."

5th grade
A fifth-grade teacher poses the following question to his students:

"How do you know that $8/10$ is equivalent to $12/15$?"

The students think for a minute and then begin writing on their whiteboards.

Becky writes, "$8/10$ is the same as $4/5$ and $12/15$ is the same as $4/5$. I can see that with my fraction strips."

Steven writes, "If you draw two rectangles and divide them up and then shade one for $8/10$ and one for $12/15$, the same is shaded."

7th grade
A seventh-grade teacher poses the following question to his students:

"How do you know that $0.4 \times 0.33 = 0.04 \times 3.3$?"

> Several students multiply the two to verify that the products are the same. They then begin discussing the question in small groups.
>
> "The numbers are the same, and the decimal points don't really matter," says Eddie.
>
> "I think the place values of the numbers are important, but I'm not really sure why," adds Annie.

Implementing the Routine

The How Do You Know? routine is easily implemented in multiple grade levels. In this routine, students are presented a question that may or may not have an obvious answer. They are given time to think about the question individually and begin to formulate an explanation. After this initial think time, the teacher may choose to give them time to talk with a partner or small group. The teacher should monitor this discussion to determine which explanations should be shared with the entire class and in what order. A wide variety of mathematical content can be used with this routine, and as a result, as students listen to the explanations of others, they have the opportunity to hear varied perspectives on many mathematical topics.

Van de Walle and Lovin (2006) provide reasons for asking students to provide explanations. One reason is that as students prepare to explain and defend their answers, they will spend more time thinking about their arguments and revising them. The chance to compare their solutions with those of others will promote greater interest in class discussions. Importantly, the explanations created in How Do You Know? place the emphasis on process and remind students that the thinking behind the answer is as important—or more so—than the answer itself.

How Do You Know? may be implemented in a variety of ways. Early in the year, teachers may choose to have the whole class work on writing an explanation of how they know the answer to a particular question. This will allow the teacher to talk with the class about the characteristics of a good mathematical explanation. (See fig. 7.1 for Deborah Ball's [2012] description of mathematical explanation.) As the children become more proficient at creating explanations, the teacher may choose to have them write explanations in pairs and then as individuals. Early elementary grade teachers may choose to have the explanations given only orally since writing explanations will probably be difficult for many students. Older students may be asked to give either oral or written explanations, and they may be asked to provide an explanation for a specific audience. For example, students could be asked to explain in written form to a first-grade student how they know that a figure is a rectangle. In addition, different tasks could be offered to students in the class to make it possible for all students to participate in the How Do You Know? routine.

Mathematical Explanation

Has a clear purpose.
- Makes clear at the outset what is being explained and why you start there; and carefully connects the explanation to the question or idea being explained.
- States what is known and what needs to be determined.

Has a logical structure.
- Summarizes at the end what has been explained and links that back to the original question, claim, or problem.

Uses representations and language clearly and carefully.
- Strives to be as simple and clear as possible.
- Uses mathematical language accurately and consistently.
- Uses representation(s) accurately.

Focuses on meaning and is geared to the learner.
- Shows what something means or why it is true and is convincing to the person to whom you are explaining.
- Takes into account the background knowledge of the listener/reader.
- Uses words that will be understood by the listener/reader.
- Breaks things down—does not assume the listener/reader knows what you are thinking.

Fig. 7.1.
Mathematical explanation (Ball 2012)

An important part of the routine is the time spent sharing explanations. This time will allow the teacher to help the students understand the components of an explanation and will enable him or her to provide support as the students practice incorporating these components. Sharing may be done first in pairs or small groups to help build confidence in children. As explanations are shared, students can be asked to look for the components of good explanations in their own explanations and those of other students. As a student is providing an explanation, fellow classmates should be encouraged to ask questions to clarify the explanation.

Another important part of the How Do You Know? routine is maintaining an ongoing record of student work on the routine. Students could write their answers to How Do You Know? questions in an individual journal so that their growth can be monitored by both themselves and the teacher. Students may also enjoy creating videos of their explanations. These could be kept as an ongoing record that students can look back at throughout the year.

Mathematical Content and Practices

Because How Do You Know? questions can be written for any mathematical content, the routine works throughout the year and in all grades. For example, young students may be asked how they know 12 is an even number, how they know 4 tens and 6 ones is the same as 46 ones, or how they know a shape is a square. Older students may be asked how they know there are not 12 square inches in a square foot, how they know a triangle can't have two right angles, how they know 500 is not evenly divisible by 3, or how they know that a sum of 7 is more likely than a sum of 11 if two dice are rolled and the numbers rolled are added.

The Common Core State Standards for Mathematics (CCSSM; National Governors Association Center for Best Practices and Council of Chief State School Officers 2010) include eight Standards for Mathematical Practice that describe the expertise teachers at all grade levels should seek to develop in their students (see appendix A). Many practices described in CCSSM may be developed through this routine. One practice states that students should construct viable arguments and critique the reasoning of others: the routine offers valuable experience with this practice for students. Students proficient with this practice can explain what to do to solve a problem and why the solution works. They will also be able to make sense of and evaluate the thinking and explanations of other students. At the elementary level, students are encouraged to use concrete objects, drawings, diagrams, and even actions to aid in their explanations. The routine will also support the development of another mathematical practice, reasoning both abstractly and quantitatively, since students will be using reasoning as they craft their explanations. The mathematical practice of attending to precision is also supported by the How Do You Know? routine. Although precision in computation is part of this practice, precision also refers to precision in verbal and written communication of mathematics. As students create and present their explanations for How Do You Know?, they will have the opportunity to develop precision in mathematical communication.

Assessing Student Thinking

Explanations provide a much clearer picture of student understanding and comprehension than do simple computational tasks. Consequently, the How Do You Know? routine provides a wonderful opportunity for teachers to assess the level of understanding of students. For example, we asked students at a variety of grade levels to explain how they knew the shape in figure 7.2 was a rectangle. We were interested in learning how they were thinking about geometric shapes and were particularly interested in determining the van Hiele level at which they were working. The van Hiele levels of geometric thought describe the thinking processes used with geometry in a five-level hierarchy. The hierarchy depicts how those at each level think and what ideas they think about rather than the amount of knowledge they have (Van de Walle and Lovin 2006). Figure 7.3 provides information about the first three levels of the model—the levels at which most elementary and middle school students work. The explanations students give with How Do You Know? provide insight into the level at which they are working. (See fig. 7.4 for examples of student work.)

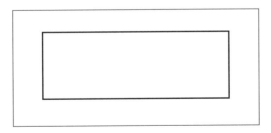

Fig. 7.2.
Figure shown to students

First Three Levels of van Hiele Model of Geometric Thought

Level 1: Reasoning by Resemblance

At this level, descriptions of and reasoning about shapes is guided by the appearance of the shape. Students will identify shapes by using the phrase "looks like." Students may be aware of the properties of geometric objects, but they do not use these properties to identify the objects.

Level 2: Reasoning by Attributes

At this level, students go beyond appearance and identify and describe shapes by their attributes. For example, a four-sided figure is classified by students as a quadrilateral because of the four sides. Students at this level often list all the attributes of a figure. However, students do not look at relationships among figures. An example of this is seen in the student who argues that a square is not a rectangle.

Level 3: Reasoning by Properties

At this level, students see the many attributes of shapes and the relationships among these shapes. Students at this level see that squares and rhombi have many properties in common. This enables students to understand that a square is a rhombus with one additional property.

Fig. 7.3.

First three levels of van Hiele model (adapted from Bassarear 2012, p. 485)

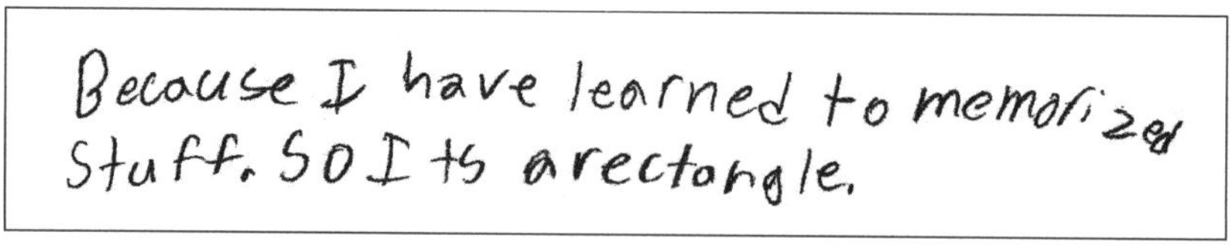

Because I have learned to memorize stuff. So I ts a rectongle.

Fig. 7.4a.

This student appears to be working at the first van Hiele level since no attributes are mentioned.

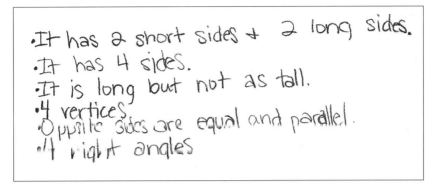

Fig. 7.4b.

This student appears to be working at the second van Hiele level since many attributes are listed. However, some of the attributes are not needed for identification of rectangles.

> It has four sides and 4 right angles.

Fig. 7.4c.

This student may be beginning to work at the third van Hiele level since not all attributes are listed, and no mention is made of the different side lengths.

Using other mathematical content to create How Do You Know? questions also provides the opportunity for students to provide mathematical explanations. Figures 7.5 and 7.6 show examples of student responses to the following questions.

- How do you know that $0.4 \times 0.33 = 0.04 \times 3.3$?

- How do you know that $8/10 = 12/15$?

> Decimals position does not matter in multiplication

Fig. 7.5a.

Seventh-grade students provide explanations for how they know that $0.4 \times 0.33 = 0.04 \times 3.3$. Each explanation offers valuable insight into student understandings and misunderstandings.

69

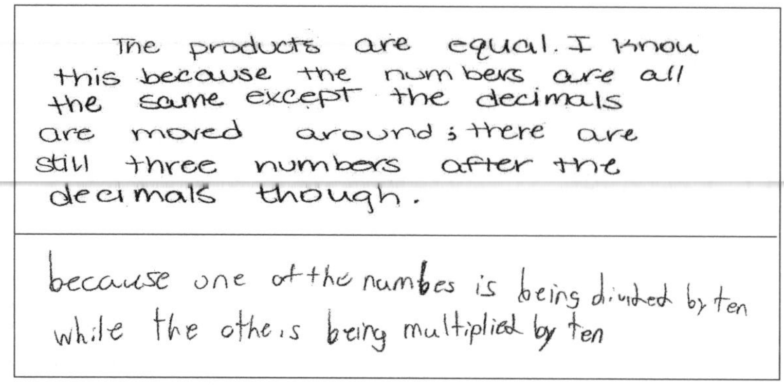

> The products are equal. I know this because the numbers are all the same except the decimals are moved around; there are still three numbers after the decimals though.

> because one of the numbers is being divided by ten while the other is being multiplied by ten

Fig. 7.5b and 7.5c.

Seventh-grade students provide explanations for how they know that $0.4 \times 0.33 = 0.04 \times 3.3$. Each explanation offers valuable insight into student understandings and misunderstandings.

Adapting the Routine

How Do You Know? is a flexible routine that is accessible to students working at a variety of levels. The cognitive demands of the routine may be altered by changing the question posed. Teachers can draft questions at various levels that are based on the same mathematical content to make the task accessible to all. For example, if the How Do You Know? task deals with explaining equivalent fractions, some students could be asked to think about $1/2$ and $3/6$, whereas others are asked to think about $8/10$ and $12/15$. These alternatives could be assigned by the teacher or they could be presented for student choice. Students may be required to use a diagram with their explanation, or they could be required to use only words. Finally, the cognitive demand could be increased by asking students to write their explanations with a specific audience in mind. For example, sixth-grade students could be asked to provide an explanation for a group of second graders. Such a requirement will cause students to think deeply about how to best present an explanation.

Conclusion

How Do You Know? is an easily implemented mathematical routine that leads to increased proficiency with mathematical explanation for a variety of mathematical topics. Because the routine can be used with any mathematical content and explanations can be oral or written, How Do You Know? can be used throughout the school year and with multiple grade levels.

The sharing of explanations created through How Do You Know? promotes precision in mathematical communication and reasoning. In addition, as students create and share their explanations, teachers have the opportunity to assess the thinking of their students.

References

Ball, Deborah L. "Practicing the Common Core: What is the Work of Teaching?" Presentation at National Council of Supervisors of Mathematics Annual Meeting, Philadelphia, Pa., April 2012.

Bassarear, Tom. *Mathematics for Elementary School Teachers*. 5th ed. Belmont, Calif.: Brooks/Cole, Cengage, 2012.

National Governors Association Center for Best Practices (NGA Center) and Council of Chief State School Officers (CCSSO). *Common Core State Standards for Mathematics. Common Core State Standards (College- and Career-Readiness Standards and K–12 Standards in English Language Arts and Math)*. Washington, D.C.: NGA Center and CCSSO, 2010. http://www.corestandards.org/.

Van de Walle, John A., and LouAnn H. Lovin. *Teaching Student-Centered Mathematics, Grades 5–8*. Boston: Pearson Education, 2006.

8

Infusing Mathematics into Nonmathematical Routines

2nd grade It's time for recess for a second-grade class. Brian checks the Classroom Jobs chart and notices that it's his day to take a basketball outside. Zach, the line leader, takes his place by the classroom door. Their teacher looks around the room and notices that the students in one row have put away all their belongings. She asks them to line up and then looks for another row that's ready. When all the students are in line, she gives Zach a signal, and he leads the class from the room. He stops when he gets to the door leading to the playground and waits for his teacher. When the teacher reaches the front of the line, she waits until all students are quiet and then dismisses the class to go outside for recess.

A routine is defined as a course of action followed regularly or a standard procedure. Our classrooms are filled with routines. Some of the routines are mathematical, such as those described in the previous chapters of this book. However, many of the routines are not mathematical and are, instead, organizational in nature—for example, procedures for taking attendance and lunch count, procedures for lining up, and procedures for transitioning between activities. Organizational routines are certainly necessary, because they build a sense of community and establish a safe learning environment. They provide feelings of predictability that lead to support in taking risks and trying new things (Shumway 2011). However, these routines do take valuable time that could be used to enhance learning. With a bit of creativity on the part of the teacher, these routines can be infused with mathematics.

Routines for Lining Up

During a school day, students make many transitions from one activity to another or from one classroom to another. The routine of lining up to go to lunch, recess, or a special class can be used to provide practice with mathematical concepts and skills:

- Students could be asked to begin writing the multiples of five starting with zero. After a brief period, the teacher will ask the students to stop. Then, he or she might ask those who stopped writing at 20 to line up first, then those who stopped writing at 35, and so on. Alternating the sequence in which students are called to the line will allow all students in the class the chance to be the first in line.

- Students could be asked to draw their favorite polygon on a sheet of a paper. They could then be asked to line up by the number of sides of the polygon drawn. For example, those who drew pentagons might be asked to line up first, followed by those who drew octagons.

- The teacher could select a mystery number and have each student write down his or her guess for what mystery number was selected. After announcing the mystery number, the teacher could ask students to line up based on how close each was to the mystery number. For instance, those who guessed 2 higher or 2 lower than the mystery number could be asked to line up first.

- Older students could be asked to determine how many prime numbers are in their telephone numbers. Those with three primes might be allowed to line up first, followed by those with one prime, and so on.

- Each student desk could be assigned an ordered pair. If the desks are in rows, the back left corner desk could become the origin, (0, 0). The desks along the back row would then represent points on the x-axis—(1, 0), (2, 0), and so forth. The desks in the left row would represent points on the y-axis—(0, 1), (0, 2), and so forth. Ordered pairs could randomly be selected to determine the order in which students line up. For middle-grades students, the teacher might choose to present an equation, and all students whose desk ordered pair represented a solution to that equation could line up first.

Routines for Standing in Line

Whether it's standing in line for lunch, standing in line to leave the classroom, or standing in line for the restroom, students spend several minutes each day waiting in line. This time in line can be put to good use with a bit of teacher creativity.

- While standing in line, the students could be asked to skip-count by a particular number from any given starting point. For example, the class could be asked to skip-count by 3s starting with 15. As a variation, the class could be asked to name prime numbers. This could be a whole-class count or each student could be asked to provide one number as the count moved down the line.

- Students could be asked to create a mathematical alphabet. The first person in line must suggest a mathematics word that starts with *A*, the second person could be asked to suggest a word that starts with *B*, and so on. This could also be done as a whole class or with partners.

- Rock–scissors–paper computation could be played as students wait in line. Students are asked to play the game with a person standing next to them. A procedure similar to rock–scissors–paper is used as students tap a closed fist onto their opposite palm and count 1, 2, 3. On the count of 3, students will flash a number of fingers. The winner may be determined in a variety of ways. Perhaps the student who flashed the larger or the smaller number could be declared the winner. Perhaps the winner could be the first person to multiply the two numbers and provide the correct answer.

- Students could be asked to silently begin counting by 5s. As they leave the room or pass by the teacher, they are asked to whisper how far they were able to count. This practice provides some informal assessment information for the teacher, as well.

- The teacher could write a mental math computation problem or a mathematics vocabulary word on a small whiteboard. Each student is asked to come up with an answer. As he or she leaves the room or passes by the teacher, the student will whisper the answer in the teacher's ear. When incorrect answers are given, the teacher may choose to have the student get back in line and try again or may choose to simply and quickly explain the correct answer.

Routines for Calling the Class Together

During mathematics lessons and work time, students are often asked to work and discuss together. Getting the attention of the entire class can be a challenge, and many teachers have specific routines, including a quiet signal or a countdown timer. Some variations on these routines can be used to infuse mathematics.

- The teacher could choose to clap a pattern. As students hear the pattern being clapped, they are to stop working and talking and repeat the clapped pattern. The teacher may need to clap two or three patterns to allow all students to hear and join in.

- A prime number countdown could be used. The teacher could start slowly naming prime numbers in reverse order. For example, "13, 11, 7, 5, 3, 2." The students are to join in as they hear the count, and all are expected to have joined in before the count reaches 2.

- The teacher may choose to establish a routine in which he or she begins listing the multiples of a number. For example, the teacher could say, "4, 8, 12, 16, ..." The students are expected to join in, and the teacher will stop the count when all are participating.

Routines for Creating Seating Arrangements

Assigning seats for students is another ideal opportunity to provide practice with mathematical concepts and skills.

- Young students often are called to a carpeted classroom area for whole-group discussions or work. The teacher could place numbers at different locations on the carpet. Each student could be given a card with a math problem on it; he or she is to sit on the carpet on top of the number that matches the answer. As students take their seats, they will hand the teacher their cards. These cards can then be used again to seat students. This procedure will help with the problem of students wanting to sit only with friends.

- Each desk in the room could be labeled with a number. As students enter the room, they are given a card with a math problem on it. They are to sit in the desk labeled with the number that matches the answer to the problem.

- Labeling each desk with an ordered pair also provides a variety of ways to seat students. If the desks are in rows, the back left corner desk could become the origin, (0, 0). This desk should be labeled with the coordinates (0, 0). The desks along the back row would then represent points on the x-axis—(1, 0), (2, 0), and so forth. The desks in the left row would represent points on the y-axis—(0, 1), (0, 2), and so forth. Other desks would have coordinates determined according to their relationship to the origin and the two axes. As students enter the room, they could be provided a card with an ordered pair on it. They are to find the desk that represents the ordered pair on the card and that desk is where they are to sit. For older students, the teacher could provide a card with an equation and an x-coordinate provided. The students will use the given x-coordinate to determine the y-coordinate and then use those coordinates to find their seats.

Your Turn!

What creative ideas do you have for making the nonmathematical routines of your classroom more mathematical?

Reference

Shumway, Jessica F. *Number Sense Routines: Building Numerical Literacy Every Day in Grades K–3*. Portland, Maine: Stenhouse Publishers, 2011.

9

High Yield from Routines

1st–3rd grade

A group of first-, second-, and third-grade teachers are meeting after school. All the teachers have collected work their students have done for the Mystery Number routine. The teachers exchange work across grade levels and continue exchanging until each has had the chance to see the work from all other teachers.

The teachers notice some similarities across all grade levels. Some students at each grade level struggle with writing a sequence of clues that allows their classmates to find the Mystery Number without providing unnecessary clues. Other students at each grade level limit their clues to those dealing with magnitude. There are also many noticeable differences. The work of the third-grade students in general displays more sophistication in the clue sequence and more consistent use of correct vocabulary.

The teachers decide to continue to focus on the Mystery Number routine because of the enhanced number sense they are noticing in students. They also decide to spend the next month focusing on the mathematical practice of attending to precision in mathematical communication. The teachers work together to plan the numbers used with Mystery Number at each grade level as well as the implementation strategies. They decide to meet again in a month to discuss how their plans worked.

Implementing mathematical routines yields positive results for both students and teachers. Routines provide access to big ideas and promote the effective use of mathematical practices and problem-solving strategies. Because mathematical routines are flexible, a wide variety of mathematical content can be used within the routine. In addition, the consistent use of common strategies across grade levels promotes coherence in and articulation of the mathematics program. The routines provide opportunities for students to demonstrate their thinking processes and for teachers to gain insight into those processes.

To maximize the mathematical yield of routines, consistent use is essential. Choosing a few routines to implement on an ongoing basis and using the routines across grade levels will increase the yield of the routines. The routines in the preceding chapters can be used with and will support any curriculum or textbook. Careful planning of the content to be incorporated into the routine will also increase student learning through the routines.

Routines as Part of Professional Development

Mathematical routines can also yield benefits in terms of professional development for teachers. School teams can meet to analyze student work for a single grade level or across grade levels. This work can provide information to teachers regarding the progression of student thinking across grade levels. Time spent analyzing the work together builds cohesion among teachers working at the same grade level and within the school.

Sztajn and colleagues, in *Supporting Implementation of the Common Core State Standards for Mathematics: Recommendations for Professional Development* (2011), offer recommendations for planning professional development designed to help teachers meet the challenge presented by the content and practice standards of the Common Core State Standards for Mathematics (CCSSI 2010). One of these recommendations is for professional development to be based on features that support teacher learning. This recommendation calls for professional development that focuses on student learning, addresses teaching specific content, and builds strong working relationships among teachers. Group meetings to discuss implementing routines and evaluating the work that results from the routines meet each of these criteria.

A second recommendation is that professional development should emphasize the substance of the Common Core. Specifically, professional development should focus on how students develop mathematical ideas over time and how the mathematical practices support learning content. As students complete the routines, they will have multiple opportunities to gain experience and expertise with the mathematical practices. As teachers plan for the implementation of mathematical routines across grades, they will learn how to incorporate and promote the eight mathematical practices described in the Standards for Mathematical Practice in the Common Core State Standards (National Governors Association Center for Best Practices and Council of Chief State School Officers 2010; see appendix A). In fact, they themselves will be using the mathematical practices as they work with other teachers on the implementation of routines.

Just a Starting Point

The routines in previous chapters of this book are meant to be a starting point. We hope that reading about the routines we describe sparks your imagination and creativity.

Resources

National Governors Association Center for Best Practices (NGA Center) and Council of Chief State School Officers (CCSSO). *Common Core State Standards for Mathematics. Common Core State Standards (College- and Career-Readiness Standards and K–12 Standards in English Language Arts and Math).* Washington, D.C.: NGA Center and CCSSO, 2010. http://www.corestandards.org/.

Sztajn, Paola, Karen Marrongelle, Peg Smith, and Bonnie Melton. *Supporting Implementation of the Common Core State Standards for Mathematics: Recommendations for Professional Development* (summary report). The William and Ida Friday Institute for Educational Innovation at the North Carolina State University College of Education, March 2011. http://www.nctm.org/uploadedFiles/Math_Standards/Summary_PD_CCSSMath.pdf.

Standards for Mathematical Practice

CCSS.Math. Practice.MP1

Make sense of problems and persevere in solving them.

Mathematically proficient students start by explaining to themselves the meaning of a problem and looking for entry points to its solution. They analyze givens, constraints, relationships, and goals. They make conjectures about the form and meaning of the solution and plan a solution pathway rather than simply jumping into a solution attempt. They consider analogous problems, and try special cases and simpler forms of the original problem in order to gain insight into its solution. They monitor and evaluate their progress and change course if necessary. Older students might, depending on the context of the problem, transform algebraic expressions or change the viewing window on their graphing calculator to get the information they need. Mathematically proficient students can explain correspondences between equations, verbal descriptions, tables, and graphs or draw diagrams of important features and relationships, graph data, and search for regularity or trends. Younger students might rely on using concrete objects or pictures to help conceptualize and solve a problem. Mathematically proficient students check their answers to problems using a different method, and they continually ask themselves, "Does this make sense?" They can understand the approaches of others to solving complex problems and identify correspondences between different approaches.

CCSS.Math. Practice.MP2

Reason abstractly and quantitatively.

Mathematically proficient students make sense of quantities and their relationships in problem situations. They bring two complementary abilities to bear on problems involving quantitative relationships: the ability to *decontextualize*—to abstract a given situation and represent it symbolically and manipulate the representing symbols as if they have a life of their own, without necessarily attending to their referents—and the ability to *contextualize*, to pause as needed during the manipulation process in order to probe into the referents for the symbols involved. Quantitative reasoning entails habits of creating a coherent representation of the problem at hand; considering the units involved; attending to the meaning of quantities, not just how to compute them; and knowing and flexibly using different properties of operations and objects.

CCSS.Math. Practice.MP3 — *Construct viable arguments and critique the reasoning of others.*

Mathematically proficient students understand and use stated assumptions, definitions, and previously established results in constructing arguments. They make conjectures and build a logical progression of statements to explore the truth of their conjectures. They are able to analyze situations by breaking them into cases, and can recognize and use counterexamples. They justify their conclusions, communicate them to others, and respond to the arguments of others. They reason inductively about data, making plausible arguments that take into account the context from which the data arose. Mathematically proficient students are also able to compare the effectiveness of two plausible arguments, distinguish correct logic or reasoning from that which is flawed, and—if there is a flaw in an argument—explain what it is. Elementary students can construct arguments using concrete referents such as objects, drawings, diagrams, and actions. Such arguments can make sense and be correct, even though they are not generalized or made formal until later grades. Later, students learn to determine domains to which an argument applies. Students at all grades can listen or read the arguments of others, decide whether they make sense, and ask useful questions to clarify or improve the arguments.

CCSS.Math. Practice.MP4 — *Model with mathematics.*

Mathematically proficient students can apply the mathematics they know to solve problems arising in everyday life, society, and the workplace. In early grades, this might be as simple as writing an addition equation to describe a situation. In middle grades, a student might apply proportional reasoning to plan a school event or analyze a problem in the community. By high school, a student might use geometry to solve a design problem or use a function to describe how one quantity of interest depends on another. Mathematically proficient students who can apply what they know are comfortable making assumptions and approximations to simplify a complicated situation, realizing that these may need revision later. They are able to identify important quantities in a practical situation and map their relationships using such tools as diagrams, two-way tables, graphs, flowcharts and formulas. They can analyze those relationships mathematically to draw conclusions. They routinely interpret their mathematical results in the context of the situation and reflect on whether the results make sense, possibly improving the model if it has not served its purpose.

CCSS.Math. Practice.MP5

Use appropriate tools strategically.

Mathematically proficient students consider the available tools when solving a mathematical problem. These tools might include pencil and paper, concrete models, a ruler, a protractor, a calculator, a spreadsheet, a computer algebra system, a statistical package, or dynamic geometry software. Proficient students are sufficiently familiar with tools appropriate for their grade or course to make sound decisions about when each of these tools might be helpful, recognizing both the insight to be gained and their limitations. For example, mathematically proficient high school students analyze graphs of functions and solutions generated using a graphing calculator. They detect possible errors by strategically using estimation and other mathematical knowledge. When making mathematical models, they know that technology can enable them to visualize the results of varying assumptions, explore consequences, and compare predictions with data. Mathematically proficient students at various grade levels are able to identify relevant external mathematical resources, such as digital content located on a website, and use them to pose or solve problems. They are able to use technological tools to explore and deepen their understanding of concepts.

CCSS.Math. Practice.MP6

Attend to precision.

Mathematically proficient students try to communicate precisely to others. They try to use clear definitions in discussion with others and in their own reasoning. They state the meaning of the symbols they choose, including using the equal sign consistently and appropriately. They are careful about specifying units of measure, and labeling axes to clarify the correspondence with quantities in a problem. They calculate accurately and efficiently, express numerical answers with a degree of precision appropriate for the problem context. In the elementary grades, students give carefully formulated explanations to each other. By the time they reach high school they have learned to examine claims and make explicit use of definitions.

CCSS.Math. Practice.MP7

Look for and make use of structure.

Mathematically proficient students look closely to discern a pattern or structure. Young students, for example, might notice that three and seven more is the same amount as seven and three more, or they may sort a collection of shapes according to how many sides the shapes have. Later, students will see 7×8 equals the well remembered $7 \times 5 + 7 \times 3$, in preparation for learning about the distributive property. In the expression $x^2 + 9x + 14$, older students can see the 14 as 2×7 and the 9 as $2 + 7$. They recognize the significance of an existing line in a geometric figure and can use the strategy of drawing an auxiliary line for solving problems. They also can step back for an overview and shift perspective. They can see complicated things, such as some algebraic expressions, as single objects or as being composed of several objects. For example, they can see $5 - 3(x - y)^2$ as 5 minus a positive number times a square and use that to realize that its value cannot be more than 5 for any real numbers x and y.

CCSS.Math. Practice.MP8

Look for and express regularity in repeated reasoning.

Mathematically proficient students notice if calculations are repeated, and look both for general methods and for shortcuts. Upper elementary students might notice when dividing 25 by 11 that they are repeating the same calculations over and over again, and conclude they have a repeating decimal. By paying attention to the calculation of slope as they repeatedly check whether points are on the line through $(1, 2)$ with slope 3, middle school students might abstract the equation $(y - 2)/(x - 1) = 3$. Noticing the regularity in the way terms cancel when expanding $(x - 1)(x + 1)$, $(x - 1)(x^2 + x + 1)$, and $(x - 1)(x^3 + x^2 + x + 1)$ might lead them to the general formula for the sum of a geometric series. As they work to solve a problem, mathematically proficient students maintain oversight of the process, while attending to the details. They continually evaluate the reasonableness of their intermediate results.